STUMBLING ALONG THE BEAT

STUMBLING ALONG THE BEAT

A Policewoman's Uncensored Story
From the World of Law Enforcement

STACY DITTRICH

KAPLAN

PUBLISHING

New York

© 2010 by Stacy Dittrich

Published by Kaplan Publishing, a division of Kaplan, Inc.
1 Liberty Plaza, 24th Floor
New York, NY 10006

Library of Congress Cataloging-in-Publication Data
Dittrich, Stacy, 1973–
Stumbling along the beat / Stacy Dittrich.
p. cm.
ISBN 978-1-60714-056-6
1. Dittrich, Stacy, 1973– 2. Policewomen–United States–Biography. 3. Sex crimes–United States–Case studies. I. Title.
HV7911.D58A3 2010
363.2092–dc22
[B]
2009040761
Printed in the United States of America
10 9 8 7 6 5 4 3 2 1

ISBN: 978-1-60714-056-6

Kaplan Publishing books are available at special quantity discounts to use for sales promotions, employee premiums, or educational purposes. For more information or to purchase books, please call the Simon & Schuster special sales department at 866-506-1949.

A police officer is a peacetime soldier always at war.

—Anonymous

There's something else besides the badge; there's a real person that's behind that, someone who cares and believes in what they're doing.

—Dennis Brown

I just observed—like when a female cop is standing with a male cop, people talk to the male cop. So women find ways to demand respect... they banter with them line for line. They shoot with them shot for shot.

—Jennifer Lopez, actress and singer

For my dad: my mentor and inspiration

CONTENTS

Contents

FOREWORD

OVER THE PAST HUNDRED YEARS or so, women have sought to even things up in predominately male work areas. Vocations and professions, which were once considered taboo or improper for women to maintain, have been slowly and grudgingly ceded to them. To the amazement of some, women were actually capable of doing the jobs of men. Since then, the female workforce has striven for recognition, equal pay, and equal opportunity—and will not be denied.

This book details the journey of one these women through the demanding and dangerous life of a law enforcement officer—and the stress, strain, and satisfaction she faced as a "woman in a man's world." I know the author very well, and am familiar with her struggles to "make her bones" and gain acceptance within the law enforcement community. She is my daughter.

Stacy grew up in a law enforcement family. I, my three brothers, and a cousin are all law enforcement officers, with more than one hundred years of collective experience. She became interested in law enforcement early in life and with her built-in tenacity, never changed course in pursuit of her goals. She eventually worked her way into a police dispatching position and worked as a telecommunicator at several levels. She took it upon herself to obtain sponsorship for the Ohio Peace Officers Training Academy, and successfully completed the requirements to become a police officer. She was sworn in to the department of a small college city as one of two female officers—eventually making detective. After years there, she was called home to the Richland County Sheriff's department in Ohio and spent the remainder of her career as a road deputy.

But this was not all Stacy accomplished. During this time, she gave birth to two lovely girls, and juggled a family while maintaining and developing her law enforcement career.

In *Stumbling Along the Beat* she shares her trials, tribulations, and successes as her career advances. Speaking as both her father and a law enforcement officer, I can assure you that you are reading the real deal. It will also soon dawn on you the Stacy is not one to hold back. What you see is what you get. She not only "talks the talk," but she has "walked the walk."

This was a very difficult book for Stacy to write. I know it brought back some ugly memories as well as some good ones. She writes from the heart and does not stray away from the truth. It is a testament to her character and her courage. In law enforcement, one of the greatest compliments an officer can get comes from his or her partners: that he or she can be counted on when the chips are down, and does not fade away in the face of danger or death. Along with her public accolades, what makes me most proud of Stacy are the many unsolicited compliments, from a variety of officers and civilians, that she is "just one of the guys." High praise indeed.

You will enjoy this book for its humanity, frankness, truth, and love.

Joseph Wendling, (Ret.) Lt. Mansfield Police Dept

December 2009

INTRODUCTION

I'M GOING TO BE VERY HONEST when I say at first I wasn't thrilled at the prospect of writing this book. In fact, I was downright horrified at the thought of it. My agent and publisher are the ones who proposed I write this; they felt my story was an entertaining one to be told.

I felt differently.

When I looked at my life, I couldn't see much there that people would want to read about—I didn't think it was all that exciting. Also, I've always been a move-forward type of person, and some of the events that happened in my past I had no desire to relive, let alone write about. But I finally relented. This book was initially meant to relay how a female police officer grappled with her job while managing a home life. I think it turned out to be much more than that. To me, it's a story of perseverance—of reaching for the brass ring when the chances of grabbing it are pretty slim. It's a story of survival, and it's a story of accepting yourself for who you are, quirks and all. Most important, it's about empowering women to keep going even when things feel hopeless. I kept going, and I fought harder than I ever had in my life until both of my hands were clenched on the brass ring. I hope my own story gives every woman that same drive and determination.

I had a lot of issues still unresolved when I began writing my story. As you'll see, there's some anger there, but there's laughter as well. I decided that if I can't laugh at myself, no one else will. And like other people, I made some pretty stupid mistakes. At the end of the last page, I realized how much writing this has helped me deal with those issues.

Probably one of the hardest decisions I had to make was whether or not to include real names and places in my stories. Sure, I could have looked at it as retribution and called these people out on the carpet, but I realized the story isn't about them—it's about me. Some of these people still work in law enforcement, have spouses and children, and although they put me through hell, I don't think it's fair to the people around them to expose them this way. There's no doubt that their identities will surface locally through the rumor mill, but that's a little different from setting them up on a world stage. I know some of them are sorry now, but the story still needed to be told. I'm sure that if they'd known their actions would have wound up in a book someday, they would have toned things down a little. We all make mistakes, and we learn from them.

Many of the stories included here came directly from years of documentation I collected as a police officer and hours of audiotapes. I never imagined I would be using them to write a book, but they certainly came in handy. Pulling all those materials out of storage brought back a flood of memories, many I didn't care to deal with. But when I came face-to-face with those memories after so many years, I did deal with them, and I've moved on.

I'm a very private person, so that made writing this book that much harder. But if I could help one woman, one *person*, achieve her dream, it was worth it. Not to mention there's nobody out there who's perfect, so be careful where the fingers are pointed.

What I put my friends and family through during the writing of this book is something that will never be forgotten. They listened to my screams, my cries, and my whining. Even my agent, Claire, didn't understand what the problem was.

"You've already written six books! This is about *your* damn life! How hard can it be to write it?" she'd say, laughing.

This was the hardest book I've ever written by far. No research, no interviews, just reaching into the past. It's funny, really; I've done countless interviews of my fictional detective series featuring the protagonist, CeeCee Gallagher. In almost every one, I'm asked, "Boy, CeeCee really seems like an alter ego of you—is she? Are *you* CeeCee Gallagher?"

I could only laugh; it was so far from the truth. CeeCee Gallagher (outside of her horrific personal life) was the cop I could only dream of being for so many years.

For the last several years, I knew something inside me had changed when it came to my career. I'd simply lost my spirit. At the end of *Stumbling Along the Beat*, I'd solved the puzzle. Those years of fighting and climbing my way to success clearly took the best out of me, and I could no longer serve the public with the compassion and dedication they truly deserve.

So now I am embarking on a new chapter, one where I tell someone else's story, or my own. I've found the compassion and dedication again, from a different perspective. It's a perspective that I can only hope will guide those who seek answers or simply want to be entertained. I will forever look back on my career with fondness, and hope that there are those out there, who will remember me for helping them through the hard times, or at best, saving their lives.

—*Stacy Dittrich*

PROLOGUE

A Long Time Ago

Although it didn't happen quite this way, it's the way I like to remember...

THE AIR WAS HOT, I was dripping with sweat, and I couldn't breathe. As I ran barefoot through the freshly mown grass, the thought of stepping on a bee raced through my mind, then flew out of my head the minute I came around the side of the house and saw my daddy's blue car parked in the driveway. Daddy's home! Every day he pulled in the driveway and honked his horn. *It's kind of late*, I thought as I ran in the front door, wondering what had kept him so long.

"Daddy! Daddy!" I yelled.

"Up here, Stacy baby!" he sang out from up the stairs.

I bounded up the stairway two steps at a time. By the time I got to the top, I knew my face was probably purple. I was so out of breath, I couldn't talk.

"Training for the Olympics?" My father cast his eyes in my direction briefly as he asked the question, then returned his attention to the bathroom mirror. He was shaving off his mustache, and I knew what that meant. I sucked in as much air as I could and blew it out, finally able to talk.

"Find another stiff today? Must've been a stinker!" I said this as conversationally as I could.

My father, who'd been a policeman for the past fifteen years, always shaved off his mustache after he investigated a dead body, especially one that had been dead for a long time. I knew that the stink stuck to his mustache hairs, and he didn't want to smell it all day. I also knew that somewhere out in the garage lay a plastic bag with his uniform in it, waiting for Mom to take it to the dry cleaners. Daddy said that was the only way to get the smell out of them.

"Honey, don't say 'stiff.' They're people — and yes, I had one today."

"But you say 'stiff' all the time!"

Daddy rinsed his razor and looked at me with his half-smile. "Do as I say, not as I do!" It was one of Daddy's more frequently repeated mottoes.

I groaned. "Tell me! Was this one a marshmallow?"

Daddy tapped his razor into the sink and began to rinse his face off and dry it with a towel. Looking into the mirror, he said, "I don't want to talk about it today, baby."

I looked at him and noticed he seemed tired, or was it sad? I knew not to push the issue just then. I'd tried that once before, and my butt had hurt for a week. Still, even though I knew better, I had to ask one more question.

"What does a dead body smell like?" I asked quietly.

Daddy hung up the towel and said just as quietly, "There's no other smell like it. It's like trying to describe a color."

I sat there for a minute, trying to decide whether or not to get mad. I hated it when Daddy talked in riddles. Of course you can describe a color. Red is...well, red. Maybe not. Anyway, Daddy seemed sad, so I decided not to get angry.

"C'mon, baby, Mommy's making dinner; get yourself cleaned up. You look like you've been rolling in a pile of dirt all day."

And with that, he went downstairs. I washed my hands and face and started to go down after him.

"Buttwipe!" I heard from behind me.

I turned around and saw my older brother, Joey, standing there.

"Mom said you're not supposed to ask him questions like that when he gets home, you little turd!" he snarled. It was almost a yell.

"You shut up! You don't know anything—and I'm telling Mom what you called me!" I almost chanted this, with just a hint of crying.

Laughing, he put on his exaggerated trembling act, said, "Ooh, I'm scared!" and laughed his way down the stairs.

Sometimes I wanted to punch my brother in the mouth. *Just because he's eleven*, I thought, *he thinks he knows everything*.

Somehow I got through dinner without fighting with Joey. Daddy was quiet; so was Mom. I think she knew what had happened today. I overheard my dad saying something about how the little girl was only five years old. My mom yelled that she didn't want to hear that crap; all it did was make her depressed.

Later on, I asked Daddy if he would tell me some happy police stories before bedtime, bringing a smile to his face.

"Well, Stacy baby, do you want to hear about the time I chased the naked robber, or the time I split the rear of my pants in a crowd of people?"

"The naked robber!"

"Okay, go watch TV for a little bit, and I'll tell you at bedtime." He winked at me as he said this.

It's weird, though. As much as I remember the beginning of that day, what happened after that is still cloudy in my mind. I remember sitting downstairs watching television, my father's police scanner screeching in the background. It always did when he was at home. My mother never turned it on when he was at work, because she said it made her nervous. I heard yelling and screaming coming from the scanner, and I turned down the television.

"Thirty-three-fifteen, we have a ten-two en route!"—radio squawks—"Fuck the squad, three hundred! I'm taking him in my cruiser!"

Even I knew that when someone said the f-word over the scanner, things were not good. I ran upstairs, yelling.

"Daddy! Somethin's happening on the scanner, they even said fuck!"

"Stacy Ann Wendling! Watch your mouth! I'm on an important phone call," he snapped, waving me away from the kitchen.

"But, Daddy!"

Daddy stood up and told whoever he was talking to, "Please hold on for a minute."

I looked up at him pleadingly. I knew it was important, and I wanted him to take me seriously.

"Whatever it is, honey, I'm sure they'll take care of it. Now, *please!*" He nodded his head toward the door, which made me think of a chicken clucking. I knew I wouldn't get his attention then, so I went back downstairs.

Time in a seven-year-old's world is very long, at least from what I remember. It seemed like several hours after I went back downstairs before the knock at the door came. Actually, it was probably less than thirty minutes. I heard the loud knock, though I didn't think much of it. It was probably one of my uncles. My dad has three brothers, all policemen, too. He has a sister as well, but she passed on the profession.

Probably Uncle Jan, I thought. He stopped by sometimes after his shift ended and had a beer with Daddy. I remember hearing the door open, then Daddy yelling and Mommy screaming. I was scared. I ran to the top of the steps and peered around the corner. I saw two policemen and an old guy in a suit.

"They don't think he's gonna make it, Joe," said the old guy.

Daddy was bent over, holding the couch. I started crying. Mom was bent over Daddy, holding on to him, also crying.

"Who's not gonna make it?" I yelled, running to them, almost colliding with Joey, who came running down the stairs from his room.

"Uncle Jim got shot," Mom said in between sobs.

I started really bawling then. Joey started crying, too.

All I remember after that is that Daddy left and was gone all night. He was with Uncle Jan, Uncle John, and Aunt Mitzi at the hospital. Mom sat crying in the living room for half the night, on the phone to my aunt Janie, Jim's wife, getting updates on his condition.

I couldn't sleep. I kept thinking that whoever shot Uncle Jim better be dead and that if he wasn't, he would be soon. I knew my family. No one shot a Wendling and lived to tell about it.

Our family, one of the most well-known and respected in the city, almost lost one of its members that night. The good thing is that Uncle Jim survived being shot. As for the guy who shot him...well, like I said, he didn't live to tell about it.

My family get-togethers were highly idiosyncratic. We'd all pass around a photo album of creepy crime scenes that Uncle Jan often brought. My mother thought it was appalling, but it was normal for me, and my cousins and I loved it. I have at least twenty first cousins on my dad's side of the family and another twenty-three on my mother's side.

Things had changed drastically in my life by the time I turned fourteen. My parents divorced. My mom couldn't take the long nights of worrying anymore and moved back to her hometown, Cleveland. I stayed behind and lived with my dad. Joey was in his first year of college.

When I turned fifteen, we decided that I was old enough to ride with my dad in his police cruiser once a month while he was working, which was how I got my first taste of being a cop. I was deeply thankful that the police department had a citizen ride-along program that allowed me to do this, with a parent's permission, of course.

While most teenagers looked ahead and explored opportunities and pondered their career choices, I had it all figured out. After I'd graduated high school and attended several colleges, I entered the Police Academy. I sailed through and graduated as class president. The feeling was total: I had finally done it, and it was one of the best days of my life.

I'm currently retired now, and since we're finally up-to-date, here is the rest of my story.

PART I

All in the Family

CHAPTER 1

Born Blue

WHAT YOU SEE is what you get. I don't have "layers," and there's nothing mysterious about me. I've sailed through life by the seat of my polyester uniform pants, appreciating the fact that I've always been a straight shooter—no pun intended.

I've had people refer to my upbringing as "unique." That may be, but after having a career in law enforcement for so many years, I believe my upbringing was no more "unique" than anyone else's.

My family is extremely large. I have forty-three first cousins on both sides. It's really not a surprise; my mother hails from a large Irish Catholic family of five kids, and my father comes from a German Catholic family of five kids. I'm pretty sure I have a first cousin in every city across the country (sure saves me plenty on hotel rooms!). Something that was slightly different from other families was that all of the men in my parents' families were cops.

My father had three brothers, John, Jan, and Jim. All four of them went to Vietnam right after high school. Their cousin Gordon followed as well. When they returned, it was a no-brainer (to them) that they would become cops. In 1969, my father entered the Police Academy, which was basically eight hours a day for a couple of weeks at the local YMCA. By the mid-1970s, there were five Wendlings in the Mansfield Police Department. Of course, this was before my uncle Jim was shot. My mother's two brothers also joined their local police forces in the Cleveland area.

I never thought my childhood was different. In fact, I look back at those years with longing, almost wishing I could cata-pult myself back in time and remain there. From my earliest memories, everything was about law enforcement. Our family was very close, as brothers should be. Most weekends, we would pack up and head to our grandparents' farm to spend the day with my aunts, uncles, and cousins shooting a vari-ety of guns at those innocent pop cans that were guilty only of being colorful targets. I shot my first gun when I was four years old, and I remember it well. It was a small .38, a revolver, and after hours of hearing my dad teach us the safety rules of guns, it was my first time to shoot. Dad stood directly behind me, arranging my hands to hold the grip properly. I had a bullet in each ear (makeshift earplugs) and pulled the trig-ger—*bam!* I actually hit the pop can and was eager to shoot more. Sometimes, when we weren't playing Dirty Harry in the woods, my grandfather Joe would take us up in his planes. A World War II pilot, "Daddy Joe," as we affectionately called him, had two small planes that were better than being on any roller coaster.

My grandfather had a unique history outside of being a war hero. When his family came to America, they ultimately settled in a predominantly German city in Ohio—Steubenville. Growing up as a teenager, he befriended a local Italian kid known then as Dino Crocetti. The world would later know him as the famous actor and singer Dean Martin. One of the more humorous stories of their friendship came when they had a falling-out and my grandfather punched Dean out cold. Dean later would say, "I never knew a man that packed a punch like Joe Wendling did back in Steubenville." After the war ended, my grandfather left Steubenville and took a factory job in Mansfield, Ohio. Shortly after his arrival, he noticed a statuesque raven-haired beauty who had the eye of every man in town. A cousin of Claudette Colbert, the famous actress from the 1940s, my grandmother Jean was immediately smitten with the handsome newcomer. They married exactly three weeks later, had four sons and one daughter, and remained married until my grandfather's death in 1985.

My own parents were one of the "Vietnam couples." They started dating in high school, my father went off to war while my mother, Susan, waited, and they married as soon as he returned—one month after she graduated from high school in 1968. My brother, Joseph III, was born the following May. While my father patrolled the streets of Mansfield, my mother was slowly working her way through nursing school, where she would ultimately become a registered nurse. Between my mother studying for her nursing exams and my father working constantly, I had a lot of time on my hands and a pretty large and vivid imagination. I used to wait anxiously for my father to come home at night so I could hear all the gritty police stories of the day.

I used those stories to investigate my own "crimes." My father had given me a hand-me-down microscope set and old handcuffs, so there were many days where I set off to catch the bad guy. I'm sure I did more autopsies on bugs using my handy microscope than any working entomologist, I'm proud to say. I'd spend hours collecting evidence, cutting off wings, and formulating theories: "The cause of death is strangulation!" Perhaps I'm most proud of the achievement I made by age ten. For hours, I would handcuff myself and try to figure a way out of them. Finally, I used my own hair barrette to slip in between the teeth of the handcuffs and slide it out. Eureka! I showed my dad, and I'm pretty sure even he was impressed.

My father always has and always will be the light of my life and the greatest hero and mentor imaginable. I strove to be like him in every way. He is the type of peson who can walk into a public place and know 90 percent of the people in there by name. He is friendly and funny, and people like him. He is nonmaterialistic, is blind to social class and race, and looks at everyone as an equal. These qualities in my father filled me with a sense of overwhelming pride. I took any opportunity I had to show him off. In Girl Scouts, for instance, when each of us was given a chance to decide where the entire troop would go on a field trip, I chose to take the troop to my dad's police department. We got to tour the jail cells and even stand inside the padded cell reserved only for the mentally disturbed. It made me proud to have him walk us through as our tour guide.

ANOTHER EXAMPLE of my attempts to be just like my father was how hard I worked to mimic the way he would raise an eyebrow at me if I did or said something wrong. I spent hours, days, weeks, in front of a mirror learning how to raise my own eyebrow. When I was finally able to do it, I literally beamed.

On holidays like Halloween, I did my best to incorporate law enforcement into the festivities, although I'd mix it up a bit: zombie cop, ghost cop, vampire cop. Law enforcement was my life. Of course, like most little girls I went through a long phase of dreaming about becoming a famous actress, model, or rock star. My mother did her best to guide me in that direction, having me model for local department stores at the age of five, but it just never seemed to fit "me." I continued down this path for a while, as you'll read later in the book, but came to the realization that no one can simply ignore who they are or what their purpose is. When I look back, it's the little things that remind me of that.

I'm sure my parents felt there was something bigger in the cards for me when I began reading by age three. When I started school, my high grades came easily (until high school, when I no longer cared—my rebellious stage). By second grade, I jumped on the Judy Blume book fad but found I could read those in a matter of hours. And they didn't challenge me.

My father had been reading Ann Rule's *The Stranger Beside*

Me, the story of serial killer Ted Bundy. I saw it sitting by his chair one day; I picked it up, read the back cover, and scurried off to my bedroom with it. My parents didn't know, or they would undoubtedly have been livid. If they came into my room when I was reading it, I'd slide the book under my pillow and pick up the decoy Judy Blume book I had next to me. I was only eight years old, and I holed up with that book for hours and finished it within several days. I was utterly fascinated with the criminal mind, but I also knew I would never quite understand it. I wanted to call Ted Bundy and ask him a slew of questions. Why did you do that? What was going through your mind? When you went to sleep at night, what did you think about? The thought of becoming an ace investigator and catching an infamous serial killer felt like Christmas morning to me. That was when I knew I would eventually be one of those "investigators." Of course, at the time, I never dreamed I'd be writing about it later or writing true crime books about people like Ted Bundy. I've told this story more times than I can count, but it sets the stage for the rest of my life; it is the beginning point that I eventually circle back to.

When my father cleaned out his desk at work and brought boxes home, I dug through them and found pictures of the most horrific homicides, suicides, or accidental deaths one could imagine. At the time, I thought it was "cool." But as you'll read later on, the "coolness" of it all wore away quickly. Again, I took every opportunity I had to delve into law enforcement. In the sixth grade, I wrote a haunting story for English class titled "The Corpse." I received an A for my use of descriptive adjectives and still have the paper to this day. In high school, I snuck a recently found homicide photo into class and showed it around. The result was a detention and serious grounding. Nowadays, a kid like me would likely raise the suspicions of Child Protective Services, maybe cause them to wonder whether I would turn out to be an early version of Eileen Wuornos. Back then, though, everyone knew where I came from. *She's a cop's kid, what do you expect?* Most of them laughed or simply shook their heads.

My poor father was oblivious to my secret investigations or thefts of his crime scene photos; after he and my mother divorced I lived with him, and he worked a lot. He worked the night shift and a lot of overtime so I could have the things most of my friends had: a car, homecoming and prom dresses, spring breaks in Florida, and so on. It wasn't uncommon for him to leave for work at five o'clock in the evening and not return until seven the next morning. That's a lot of free time for a teenage girl. He did the best he could, and frankly, I don't think I turned out bad at all. They way I look at it is, yes, I snuck some gruesome photos into school, read true crime under the covers, and got kicked off the cheerleading squad for smoking a cigarette in my high school bathroom. But I never got pregnant, did drugs, dropped out of school, or became an all-around delinquent. Considering the freedom I had, I'd say that was a hell of an accomplishment.

I'm sure my father feels the same way.

There were some touch-and-go incidents in that time, incidents that I'm sure caused the majority of my father's gray hairs.

For instance, there was a time when I had just gotten off work from my high school job at a frozen yogurt shop. It was late; I was tired and anxious to go home. After peeling out of the parking lot, I cranked up my stereo and began to cruise along. I had gone at least six or seven miles when I finally took a look in my rearview mirror and saw the flashing lights behind me. Thinking it was a cruiser going to a call, I pulled to the side of the road to let him pass by. It was then I saw the nine or ten other police cars stop directly behind me: state highway patrol and deputy sheriff cruisers. It dawned on me what had happened. I had just become a suspect in a vehicle pursuit. Apparently, right when I pulled out of work a state trooper turned on me and tried to pull me over for speeding. Since I wasn't paying attention, I just kept cruising along, singing my heart out to Bon Jovi.

Realizing what I had just done, I slowly put up my hands and started bawling. By the time the first trooper got to my window, I was almost hysterical. Funny, the trooper had something of a smirk on his face when he started talking.

"You Joe Wendling's kid?" was the first thing he asked.

All I could do was nod.

"You want to tell me why you didn't stop?"

"I wasn't paying attention," I said through my sobs. "I had my radio on and never even looked in my mirror. I'm sorry!"

"Well, I figured something wasn't right." He smiled. "I know your dad, and this car's registration returns to him...not to mention I've never been in a pursuit that was only going forty miles an hour by a young blonde with a ponytail. But I had to call it in anyway since I wasn't sure. We called your dad; he's waiting for you at home. You okay to drive?"

Another nod.

"Consider this a warning. I had you at thirty-nine in a twenty-five-mile-per-hour zone when I first tried to stop you. And a stern warning to start looking in your rearview, young lady."

I was completely stunned that I wasn't going to jail, let alone getting a ticket. This time, when I looked in the rearview mirror, I saw all of the cops laughing it up. Fine by me; I was more than happy to be their humor for the day—at least I was going home.

My dad was standing at the front door waiting when I got home. Needless to say, I lost my driving privileges for a few weeks after that.

As if that incident weren't bad enough, I snuck out one night with several guys and gals. One of the guys worked at an athletic club that included a pool, so we essentially trespassed there, swimming and drinking beer. On our way home, we were stopped downtown at a red light with one car in front of us. The next thing I knew, about twenty police cars swarmed all around us; cops jumped out, guns pointed, screaming at us, "Let me see your hands!" All I know is I looked to my right and the nearest cop standing there pointing a gun at our car was my dad. I literally came unglued. Like an idiot, I dropped to the floorboard, screaming at the driver to go! Of course, had we truly been the focus of the felony stop—I thought we were stopped for our minor trespassing infraction—my actions would've been the worst possible thing to do. Needless to say, we realized in a split second that the focus of the guns and cops was the car directly in front of us. I later learned they had just committed armed robbery in a nearby convenience store.

Actually, I was so upset by this incident that I told my dad the entire story the next day. Waiting for the ultimate berating and grounding, I was shocked when he began laughing his ass off.

"That'll teach you," he said before he handed down my punishment of two weeks' grounding.

He was right: The chance of my pulling another similar stunt was close to zero.

Deciding it was best to stay out of trouble, I took advantage of the ride-along program at my father's police department. On weekends, I was able to ride with my father during his shift. Not every weekend, of course, but I jumped at the opportunity whenever I could. I remember the first time I rode, the first time I saw my father as a police officer—not the man I knew at home—and it was mind-blowing, to say the least.

Our first "hot" call was a rather large bar fight at one of the seedy drinking spots downtown. At this time, the cops were still driving the old Chevys whose engines sounded like a 747 jumbo jet taking off. We were quite a distance away from the fight, so my father floored it. I had never ridden that fast in a car, especially going around turns, over hills, with lights blaring and siren screaming. It was awesome. It beat any roller coaster I had been on up until that point, and I knew then that was definitely the kind of life I wanted.

When we arrived at the fight, my excitement turned to sheer horror in a matter of seconds. This was where I finally saw my father in his "cop mode." As we rolled up to the front of the bar, a mass of people were outside, punching and throwing one another around, with a few other cops in the mix. As my father jumped out of the car, he yelled at me, "Stay in the car!" I watched him run over to a big thug who was rolling around on the ground with another officer. As he promptly jerked the thug up and threw him to the side, I was horrified to see an extremely large—I mean fat—woman run over to my father and jump on his back. She started clawing at him every which way but sideways. It was all I could do to not jump out of the car and run over there to help him. I sat there feeling as if I were going to bawl as I watched my father being viciously attacked by a three-hundred-pound psychopathic bar whore. She wasn't there for long; he literally bent over and slammed her on the ground, yelling, "Get the fuck off of me!"

That was it. I had never in my life heard my father use the word *fuck,* nor had I ever seen him look so angry or be involved in a fight. It scared me to death! I thought, *I will never make that man angry again for the rest of my life.*

When he got back into the car and saw my wide-eyed look of terror, he started to laugh.

"Scared ya, didn't it?" he said. "Hey! You wanted to ride with me. I told you it wasn't going to be what you expected!"

"I thought you were going to get hurt!" My voice was shaking before I quieted down. "And I've never heard you use the f-word before."

His expression went from jovial to shocked. "Uh-oh, I didn't realize that...sorry, honey, but sometimes that happens."

That was my eye-opening experience to life on the street. We went to serious, not-so-serious, and life-threatening calls. As bad as some of them were, or as funny, I knew I would experience it all on my own someday.

Years later, when I graduated as president of my Police Academy, I stood before hundreds of people speaking about my path toward law enforcement and thanking my father. I knew I was about to embark on an unknown journey, a journey that would take me places I could never have imagined.

Regardless of my excitement, fears, and emotions, I welcomed the challenge.

CHAPTER 2

Tactical Barbie

*C*AN I REALLY *do this?*

Those words came shrieking through my head the day I stood inside the living room and looked at the little boy. I was a rookie, four weeks on the job and still riding two-man with my field training officer.

I was a twenty-four-year-old single mother with a one-year-old daughter and had dreamed of becoming a police officer like my father since I was a little girl. Now, I wasn't so sure. Becoming a police officer was all about the excitement for me. I used to ride with my father sometimes during his shift and learned quickly that I was an adrenaline junkie. The blaring siren, the flashing blue and red lights, and driving ninety miles per hour were was instantly addictive. After learning to shoot a pistol when I was four years old, I spent the rest of my time listening to my father and his three brothers, also cops, tell their gritty stories of the job.

However, I didn't recall hearing any exciting stories about what I stood facing that very moment. In fact, when we covered sex offenses and child molesters in the Police Academy, I naïvely assumed those cases would be handled by the seasoned detectives. I was a street cop in uniform; I wanted to go out, have fun, and kick ass. This wasn't what I signed up for.

My training officer and I had been called to a house about a problem with the neighbor. No big deal, right? Wrong. The problem—and the small redheaded four-year-old boy I stood looking at—proved to be one of the most memorable and crucial of my career. So what exactly happened?

The residence was situated in a nice, middle-class neighborhood with maple trees lining the street, kids riding their bicycles on the sidewalks, and the smell of barbecue in the air. The boy's father met us at the door to discreetly give us details of the horrific event that had just transpired. The boy had been in his backyard, playing like any normal child on a bright, sunny fall day. It had been only a few minutes when the father realized his son was no longer there and, as would any concerned parent, he went outside to investigate. Hearing noises from behind the utility shed, the father walked around the corner and saw a man who lived nearby beginning to sodomize his son.

Shocked beyond any normal man's comprehension, the father began chasing the man through the backyards, only to stop and realize his son needed him first.

"Honestly, I had to stop myself," I recalled the father saying. "If I'd caught him, I think I would have killed him."

"You had a lot more restraint than I would have," my training officer told the man. "Does your son need medical attention?"

The father shook his head. "No, he didn't...uh, he hadn't put it in yet."

The man's face, already pale, lightened two more shades as he said those words. My stomach turned, and I immediately began to feel the lump rising in my throat. *Don't do this right now!* I had to tell myself over and over in a halfhearted attempt to not break down that very minute. I didn't want to be there, and this was not why I'd become a cop. But it was part of the job, and I had to do it. That was the day I began my disgusting habit of chewing on my bottom lip to keep a stone face and hold my tears at bay.

Unfortunately, in my eyes the situation grew worse when we entered the home to speak to the man's son. I'll never forget walking into the living room and seeing the adorable little boy sitting on the couch next to his mother. The mother was just as shell-shocked as the father and wore the same ashen complexion. Both remained silent when we walked in, but I immediately noticed a tear form and run down the boy's cheek.

"Mommy, are they going to put me in jail?" the little boy whispered to his mother.

"No, honey, they're here to help," she whispered back, tears forming in her own eyes.

That did it. I excused myself from the room, told my training officer I was going to get something out of the car, and walked outside. Looking like a lunatic, no doubt, I paced back and forth in front of the porch, taking deep breaths while placing my hands on top of my head. I would not cry.

I was one of two females, the first ever, hired at the small department. Forever under the microscope, I was aware of the obstacles I faced with my male peers. If I buckled now, there would be no going back. This was what they all expected, and I'd be damned if I proved them right. I thought about my baby girl, but that just made the situation worse. I thought about the little boy inside who thought the police were there to take him away—he thought he had done something wrong. How could I possibly do this for the next twenty-five years? Had I made a mistake?

Forcing myself to get it together, I retrieved a gold sticker police badge from inside the cruiser. Taking a deep breath, I opened the door and went back inside. My training officer was taking notes and beginning the paperwork for what would be a very lengthy report. I chose to sit next to the little boy and forced a smile.

"I have something for you," I said quietly. "It's only for the most special kids, and you get one today."

I peeled off the back of the sticker and placed it gently on the boy's shirt. He looked at me, and his face broke out into a grin. "Thank you."

My partner motioned for me to join him in the next room. It was there he informed me the suspect lived only three or four houses down and that we would be going to arrest him imme-diately. The father was familiar with the suspect, a young man in his early twenties; he lived with his mother and was border-line retarded. As we approached the house, I felt my emotions clouding with anger. I wanted to be face-to-face with the man who, in a matter of seconds, had traumatized an innocent child (who would likely now need years of therapy, along with the parents) and destroyed the safe atmosphere of a once quiet neighborhood. But as shocking as the sexual assault was, what happened next almost shocked me more.

Answering the door was a tall, brown-haired man with a boyish face. Upon seeing two uniformed officers at his door, he spoke first, smiling all the while.

"I know why you're here. I did it," he said calmly.

My training officer and I looked at each other in shock. There was more to come.

"Ma! I gotta go to jail!" the man yelled behind him. "See ya!"

Recovering quickly, my training officer opened the door and told the man to step inside. We walked in behind him and saw an elderly woman seated in a rocking chair, crocheting. As my partner handcuffed the man, the woman continued to crochet as if only the mailman were there, but she asked one simple question:

"What'd he do?"

My partner explained the situation, adding that the man was going to be charged with abduction and attempted rape.

Her eyes now fixated on the television, she twirled the crochet needle in and out of the yarn like a pro.

"I tole you to knock that shit off!" she said to her son.

"I couldn't help it. Bye, Ma," he replied, still smiling.

Astounded by their responses to the situation and their interaction with each other, my training officer and I silently walked the man to the waiting police cruiser. As I placed him the backseat, I was further shocked to learn I would be driving the man to the police station alone.

"I have to go back to the house and get more statements from the parents and the victim," said my training officer. "Take him to the station and put him in one of the interview rooms. The detectives will meet you there."

As ordered, I began the drive to the station, once again feeling the lump rise to the back of my throat as I watched the smiling man in the backseat. For a moment I wanted to stop the car, drag him out, and pistol-whip him. Anger, sadness, and acceptance all intertwined on the brief ride that day. One of the more disturbing aspects of my emotions was the emotions themselves: Why was I reacting like this? My training officer had remained stoic through the entire ordeal while I'd felt like screaming. No, I wasn't going to make it through this job.

After handing the man off to the detectives, I quickly walked out of the department, got back into my car, and completely lost it. Sitting in the parking lot, sobbing, I kept looking around to make sure no one saw me. I desperately needed someone to talk to, knowing the only one who would understand would be my father.

Using my cell phone, which back then happened to be the size of a small shoebox, I sat inside my police car and called my dad. Just hearing his voice made me feel twelve years old again, essentially causing me to cry harder as I told him the story.

"I don't think I can do this, Dad!" I choked.

"Sure you can. Remember, you're a human being, and there's nothing wrong with how you're reacting." His voice was calm and soothing. "Trust me, it will get easier."

I took his word for it; with his thirty-five years on the job, he had to know what he was talking about. And from that day on, I was hell-bent on doing everything in my power to squash the sex offenders. I found myself actually thriving when dealing with them, knowing I had the ability to put them away so they couldn't hurt any more children.

Nonetheless, the crippling thought of not being able to handle the job continued to haunt me in those first six months as a rookie. In retrospect, I was a complete mess—almost laughable.

In my very first day as a police officer, I strode into the men's locker room proudly wearing my uniform. Remember, I was a pioneer female, so there wasn't a women's locker room. A large table was situated in the middle of the men's locker room, and roll call was actually held there.

I had been standing there for mere seconds when a sergeant looked me up and down. He started laughing, which drew the attention of the other officers in the room.

"What the hell did you do?" he asked.

Feeling my face burn while turning three different shades of scarlet, I was speechless since I didn't know what he was talking about. He walked over and pointed at my buttons. I had the silver brass buttons down the front of my shirt. Of course it was at that very moment that I noticed no one else had them.

"Did you cut your buttons off?"

"I thought we had to replace them with these," I whispered, humiliated.

The room erupted in laughter, but it didn't stop there. After walking in a circle around me, the sergeant tugged at my gun belt.

"Jesus Christ, you don't even have your belt keepers on right!"

Since, again, I had no idea what he was talking about, I remained silent, listening to the rebirth of laughter.

"Do you even know what those are for?" he questioned.

"I thought they were to hang keys on, sir," I replied, still whispering.

The laughter erupted again, louder this time. Apparently, the belt keepers were supposed to loop around my regular belt and my gun belt, holding them together; hence the name. Had common sense been a strong point of mine at the time, I would've figured it out. It was bad enough they had only a men's bullet-proof vest for me to wear—the thing was so large and heavy, it felt as though a school bus had landed on my chest. I began to worry that I didn't have the vest on correctly, either.

"Fuckin' Barbie," one of the guys said.

A glorious first day. Even worse, the name stuck. Soon after, my locker was wallpapered with Barbie doll stickers, and I was forever tagged "Tactical Barbie."

The "Tactical" part was added later, after the following incident: My first day on my own, after three months of field training, I was exhilarated. Working the midnight shift, I left roll call eager to get to the street and start kickin' ass. I had been on my own for approximately fifteen minutes when I saw a suspicious vehicle exit an alley without its headlights on. *I got you!* My first ever traffic stop. *I'll find drugs, they probably have warrants, I'll bet the car is stolen, the guys will think I'm great, I'll be a hero on the first day!* My thoughts raced as I exited my car and approached theirs, placing my hand on my gun as I was halfway between the cars. *You better not turn around, buddy, I'll—*

Oops—I forgot my gun.

My holster was empty, and I realized at that moment that I had left it back at the station. Brilliant. As I stood behind the suspect vehicle that had God only knew what in it, I had to quickly figure out my next course of action. I already knew I couldn't approach the driver without my gun. I would hate to make history as the first officer ever to be killed the first day.

I ran back to my car as if I were in a hurry and yelled up to the driver:

"Hey, buddy, turn your headlights on! I have an emergency I've been called to!"

I drove away from the stop like a bat out of hell, heading for the department and praying I wouldn't get dispatched to an emergency.

No such luck.

I was around the corner from the department, convinced I would make it, when I was dispatched to a domestic fight in progress. I clearly couldn't go to a dangerous call like that without my gun. I speeded up, whipped into the parking lot, and sprinted into the department, praying no one was inside to see what I had done.

It was an unlucky day.

Two officers were standing in the locker room as I flew in and retrieved my Glock .40-caliber handgun from my locker. There wasn't time to be discreet, and as I ran back out, one of them yelled,

"Did you forget your fuckin' gun?"

I was new, naïve, and clueless—a bad combination if I wanted to be an effective police officer. And my first six months as a rookie were something to behold.

At one point during my first day on the road, with my training officer, we were dispatched to a fight call.

"Go ahead and fire it up," my training officer said.

"I didn't know you smoked," was my response.

"I meant the roof! Turn on the lights and sirens." He was shaking his head.

"Oh."

Later, when our shift was over and my training partner had a chance to share our little exchange with the others, it was said during roll call that everyone was convinced that "Tactical Barbie" dyed her blond roots brown.

So yes, I stumbled through those first six months, falling down a couple of times along the way. But my father was right.

It did get better.

PART II

Life on the Beat

CHAPTER 3

Suffer the Children

I FIRMLY BELIEVE THAT people should be required to apply for a license to become parents, much as they do to drive cars, get married, and carry guns. Many parents simply have no business giving birth and raising children—it's not in their nature. Practical, ethical, and legal aspects aside, of course.

Just a small example of the parallels between nonmaternal people and animals takes me back to Christmas morning 2007, my daughter, Brooke, went outside to feed her beloved floppy-eared bunnies, Zoe and Lopsy. Our babysitter, Mindy, raised bunnies, and since we had moved into the seclusion of a state forest, the girls begged me for them. I had no experience raising or caring for any animal other than Sadie, my Labrador retriever, but I said, "Sure," as long as they remained outside, living in the woods. How hard could caring for two bunnies be?

Unbeknownst to all of us, Zoe was pregnant. Clearly, Brooke had ignored my orders to keep Zoe away from her male counterpart. Sometime during the night, Zoe had given birth to seven babies and proceeded to stomp on—and chew—each one of them to death. What Brooke found inside the cage that morning was nothing less than a slaughter, a traumatic event to an innocent eleven-year-old. I remember hearing the screams coming from outside, as did my youngest daughter, Jordyn, who was five at the time. I ran out to see what horror had caused such screaming—and immediately wished I'd at least had the foresight to keep Jordyn from running out with me. The baby bunnies (what was left of them) looked like pieces of bloody, hairless rats. Now it was my turn to scream, for my husband, Rich, as my daughters ran sobbing hysterically into the house.

That unfortunate Christmas morning was forever branded "the Baby Bunny Massacre" and Zoe the bunny was dubbed "the murderer" by my daughters. I silently renamed her Susan Smith. According to Mindy, this was the second litter Zoe had slaughtered, and there was no logical explanation for it—sometimes certain bunnies weren't cut out to care for their young. However, while animals act out of instinct, regardless of the result, some humans demonstrate—consciously and deliberately—the capacity for pure evil.

The incidence in our society of child abuse (emotional, physical, sexual) and neglect is egregious and has long represented an excessive burden on law enforcement. To ease this burden, the U.S. government authorized the establishment of a number of state agencies referred to collectively as Child Protective Services. However, although its title conjures images of a supportive and benevolent institution, the reality is anything but—indeed, some of the mistakes made by CPS nationwide are appalling. But the fact remains that the blame must first be placed on those directly responsible for the abuse.

There have been very few times in my career where, during an interview with a suspect, I wanted to reach across the table and rip out his eyes. Sounds brutal, I know, and I never did it, of course (although I certainly *imagined* it). One case that stands out involved a five-year-old boy I'll call "Sam."

Honestly, I can't remember how the complaint came in. I remember that it was an allegation of child abuse, so as a detective it was my job to investigate it. I checked with CPS to see if they had an open case on the family. They did, but their investigation had proved to be "unfounded," so they'd closed it. Apparently, their complaint consisted of allegations that Sam's mother was pulling him around the house with a dog leash. Before making contact at Sam's house, I checked with his kindergarten teacher to see if she had observed any problems with Sam. She sure had!

Every couple of days (the days he actually made it to school), Sam would come to class in jeans soiled with feces. It got so bad that the teacher kept an extra pair of jeans and underwear on hand for him to change into, and eventually this became so routine that the teacher didn't feel it was necessary to contact law enforcement. She *may* have called CPS at some point, but she couldn't remember.

My interview with Sam was gut-wrenching. I'll never forget seeing him for the first time; small for his age, he had huge brown eyes and curly brown hair, the kind of child you just want to scoop up and squeeze. He was very quiet and wouldn't look at me directly. Since I hadn't interviewed his mother yet, I got bits and pieces from him that didn't make sense. He spoke of getting swatted in his rear end with tree branches, not being allowed to sleep, and getting bloody noses. When the time came to interview his mother, "Lisa," I stayed calm, believing there were two sides to every story and wanting to hear both before reaching a conclusion. In this case, however, there was essentially one side to all of it.

When Lisa arrived for her interview, she seemed quiet, like her son. A large woman dressed in secondhand clothes, she exuded an odor that I always called "hillbilly funk." Lots of people I dealt with smelled like Lisa—a mixture of body odor, greasy hair, bad breath, and cat piss.

We sat down and began to talk about Sam's history. I already knew quite a bit, and at first, as I listened to this woman speak, I thought for sure it was all a misunderstanding; she seemed meek, timid, and somewhat kind—not the personality of your typical child abuser.

What I already knew was that Sam had been brutally raped by a neighborhood thug when he was only four. The man had taken him into the nearby woods and sodomized him several ways, one that included a tree branch. But the story went much deeper, and this was where I began to see Lisa for the monster she was.

Because of the severity of the rape, Sam sustained extensive injuries to his bowels. The doctors explained to Lisa that he would need several surgeries to repair the damage that made him unable to control his bowel movements.

"And when did he have the surgery?" I asked.

"He didn't. I ain't got no insurance," Lisa replied calmly.

Apparently, Lisa had no problem letting her son walk around defecating in his pants, nor had she made any effort to get him into counseling to deal with the psychological effects of the rape. Her nonchalant and dismissive attitude was irritating me, that and her sickening smile, as though nothing fazed her. Even better, or worse (take your pick), she was honest about everything. And casual: To listen to her tell the story, you would think you were hearing about someone's day at the grocery store.

Lisa didn't have insurance to get Sam the surgery he needed and had made no effort to acquire any public assistance.

"Too many forms I didn't understand," she said with a chuckle.

It angered her when Sam defecated in his pants. To correct the problem, this cruel, demented woman believed that by taking a tree branch—the same item he'd been sodomized with—and swatting him in the rear with it, she would fix everything. The bloody nose? Oh, well, little Sam had been hungry for breakfast and she'd wanted to sleep in, so she'd backhanded him a good one. Why did Sam miss so much school? She and her boyfriend were always up late and wanted to sleep in. On the nights they had sex, they made Sam sit at the end of the bed and watch.

"I just didn't want him to get into anything he's not supposed to," said this Mother of the Year with a smile.

But why no baths for little Sam?

"I didn't want to miss *David Letterman*!"

She even went so far as to admit to me that she had a family friend lie to the CPS caseworker about the dog leash. "Only sometimes" was little Sam forced to wear the leash. Grappling with a wave of nausea, I determined that this woman had some type of mental disability, was possibly borderline retarded. No one could sit there smiling, giggling, and twirling her hair as she discussed the brutal torture she subjected her small child to daily. I quickly grabbed the file and flipped through it. She had graduated high school and held a job—no mental disabilities there.

Ethical or not, I unleashed a verbal tirade against Lisa, using words like "fat and lazy," "stupid, worthless, filthy bag of shit," and others. To me, it was well worth a disciplinary write-up. Again, no reaction. Only one word caused her smile to fade and her eyes to open wide—prison. I honestly think that Lisa confessed everything to me because she hoped that Sam would be removed permanently from her custody. I believe that's what she wanted. It never dawned on her that she might go to prison.

Sam was placed in foster care, and I don't know what became of him. Lisa didn't know who his father was, so there was not much hope for Sam—the damage was done. His is one of the many faces that flash through my mind from time to time. Not often, but enough to make me wonder what might have become of him.

As shocking as Sam's story is, just about every cop on the beat can tell you a similar story of child abuse and neglect.

In law enforcement, the voices of the young and innocent scream at you when you least expect it. I was in uniform, patrolling the lonely streets one winter night, when I noticed the newspaper delivery lady on her route. New to the area— she had been on the route for only a couple of weeks—she always pushed an old baby stroller around with what all of us thought was filled with newspapers. Call it what you will, boredom or instinct, but I decided to stop and check the lady out. Peering over the side of the stroller, expecting to see piles of plastic-wrapped newspapers, I was shocked to discover a newborn baby inside, wearing only a thin "onesie" nightshirt. When I called our dispatchers to check the temperature, they informed me it was in the low twenties.

When the other officers heard on their radios what I was up to, they flocked to my location. Most of them felt guilty for not checking her out earlier.

"Jesus! I always thought she had newspapers in there!" was the general consensus.

We all felt guilty, but in a strange way, I felt a little sympathy for the woman. What I learned when I escorted her back to the rented room provided by the homeless shelter was that her asshole husband, a minister who'd been dismissed from his position, had forced her to get the newspaper delivery job. To make matters worse, the route began at three o'clock in the morning. Their baby was only six weeks old, so to make sure he got an uninterrupted night's sleep, he'd forced his wife to take the infant with her. They couldn't even afford warm clothing for the baby.

I did my job and issued criminal citations to both of them for child endangerment. But I knew it wouldn't go anywhere, and I was right. The law director (city prosecutor) asked me later if I would mind if they dismissed the charges. The couple didn't have a dime to their name, couldn't afford any fines, and had been adopted by a local church that was providing them with shelter, food, clothing, and child care. All was right with the world.

One of my biggest pet peeves surrounding child neglect is the way people live. That's right: living conditions. It wasn't until I became a cop that I saw just how filthy some people's homes are. And this has nothing to do with socioeconomics, race, religion, or social classification. I once went into a ten-thousand-square-foot mansion for an accidental alarm call and had to walk down "cleared" paths in between piles of garbage and dog feces that covered the home. Now, I certainly have moments where I throw my clothes and shoes wherever I feel like it, but over the years of going into some of these homes, I have acquired phobias and distastes I never had before. For instance, God help anyone who stands near me smelling of Hamburger Helper, that ever-present odor in low-income housing projects. Then there's the mother of them all—cats. I've walked into homes where the smell of cat urine and ammonia was so strong that my eyes began to water and I had to wash my uniforms two or three times just to get rid of the odor. I could be in a house like that for less than five minutes and I would smell it the rest of the day on my clothes, in my hair, and inside my cruiser. Try to imagine a child living in something like that every day.

I happened upon the crème de la crème of filth one night when I was called to a disturbance in a seedy trailer park in the northern part of the city. The neighbor had heard yelling coming from the trailer next door. For us, this sort of call was simple—basically, we knock on the door, say, "Keep it quiet; if we come back, someone is going to jail," and leave. No paperwork... a cop's dream call. However, if there's one thing in law enforcement to be learned, it's to always expect the unexpected.

Accompanied by another officer, we knocked on the door and hoped for a speedy resolution. Unfortunately, as soon as the door opened and I saw the small child in the background, I knew it wasn't going to be speedy or simple. Of course, I didn't mention that when the door opened, the smell from inside the trailer just about knocked us off the rickety steps. The noises the neighbor had heard were a husband and wife having an argument, nothing major. The reason he'd heard everything so clearly was that the trailer was full of holes. When we walked into the trailer, I almost gagged.

Garbage was strewn all over the floor—what was left of it, that is. The two large rottweilers and cats had urinated on the floor so much that it had rotted out the wood in large areas. The homeowner's solution was to put old wooden planks across the holes and throw carpet samples over them. Even worse, there were fleas everywhere. They attacked us the minute we stepped inside. I could feel them crawling inside my pant legs. Looking around the small abode and noticing the hundreds of knives and swords that hung from the walls, I snapped back to attention and focused on the two toddler girls who stood there looking at me. Wearing nothing but fully loaded diapers, the children were filthy from head to toe. The mother, apparently realizing the need for a diaper change, swiftly picked up the nearest child, laid her on the couch, and apologized for the condition of the trailer.

"I didn't have time to clean today," she said nervously.

What had accumulated inside that trailer was weeks, if not months, of filth. Regardless, I stood guard as I watched the woman peel off the child's diaper. What I saw made me recoil. The child's vaginal area was so red, swollen, and chafed that it was hard to determine what sex she was. To make matters worse, instead of reaching for the diaper wipes that sat on a shelf directly above her head, the mother grabbed a nearby filthy dishrag that was covered in dog hair and began to clean the child's vaginal area with it.

"Stop!" It was too much. "What the hell are you doing? There's diaper wipes right above your head!"

"Oh, right, I'm sorry, I forgot. I'm just a little nervous right now," she mumbled.

The two little girls were in such bad shape that we had no choice but to take them to the emergency room. We carried them out to the waiting ambulance and followed it to the hospital, where we learned that the children were covered in flea bites and suffering from scabies. Hearing this last bit of news, I could only close my eyes and groan. Scabies are extremely contagious, and any time we came in contact, we were promptly handed a Styrofoam cup of yellow disinfectant powder to take home and shower with—it's awful. After several weeks of checking continually between fingers and toes for bites, the routine becomes obsessive. Luckily, I had never contracted scabies, but whenever I came in contact with someone who had, I drove around for two days feeling the damn things crawling through my hair.

Most of these children survive because of us. Unfortunately, some do not survive the abuse or neglect, and others do survive but would have been better off dead. I know how this sounds, but after you hear what happened in the case of "baby James," you might understand.

In January 2002, I was almost seven months pregnant and feeling as if I were the size of the moon. I was still in the detective bureau and had the glorious gift of working Mondays through Fridays from nine to five. It was Saturday, my day off, and I had gotten up around seven a.m. to finish getting the nursery together. By midnight, I was exhausted and had just gotten into bed when my phone rang. It was my partner, "Dave." We were both on call, and Akron Children's Hospital had just contacted our department. A baby with critical injuries sustained in our jurisdiction had been admitted. The doctors determined the injuries had been caused by repeated and violent shaking.

So much for sleep. I threw on one of my maternity tents, and Dave and I made the hour-long drive to Akron. We didn't know much, only that the baby was pretty much on life support. I dreaded the notion of seeing an infant in such a state, especially since I was in a fairly shaky condition myself. When we arrived, we were whisked to the intensive care unit and led to the bedside of the small child who was fighting for his life. I feared I would have a visible reaction to the countless tubes and wires that ran into the small, motionless body, but, surprisingly, I didn't. In fact, it was my lack of emotion that bothered me most. Feeling my own child growing restless within me, I placed my hand on my swollen middle and thought, *Thank God this isn't my child.* I felt sympathy and a slight sadness, but mostly I was angry. Experience had taught me to suppress my emotions to do my job, and for the most part it had worked, but the anger was always hardest to control.

When we spoke to the attending physician, we heard the familiar terms that described the child's injuries: subdural hematoma, retinal detachment, and decreased brain activity. In layman's terms, a skull fracture, blindness, and brain damage.

The details of the case involving the baby turned out to be quite bizarre, actually. The child's mother, a stripper from Cincinnati, had met a guy on the Internet and moved to my jurisdiction to live with him, with baby James in tow. Apparently, the fact that this guy, Brian Patrick, was married didn't seem to faze anyone. He simply banished his wife to the basement and moved his girlfriend in: one big, happy family. The horror stories that came out after the assault on the baby were mind-blowing.

Brian Patrick was a monster; his wife could more than attest to that. She told stories of how Brian had tortured her animals whenever she'd refused to comply with his orders. Once, they were driving down the highway and she had her favorite cat in the car. Brian got angry at her over something minimal, grabbed the cat, and tossed it out the window, where it was promptly run over by several cars. In another horrific incident, this one involving a puppy his wife had just acquired, Brian got mad at something she'd said or done, grabbed the puppy, and held its mouth over the nozzle of a garden hose. With the hose on full blast, he drowned the puppy right in front of her as she stood there screaming.

When his girlfriend moved in with her baby, Brian soon found that the child's crying drove him crazy. He thought that tossing baby James up into a ceiling fan would do the trick. When that didn't work, he tossed the baby like a football into a nearby china cabinet. The fracture on the baby's skull was perfectly round from one of the brass knobs on the cabinet. This type of abuse went on for several days. One of the more stomach-churning details of the assault occurred when the child's mother noticed the baby's eyes were crossed. Brian held the baby down and, with his finger, tried manually to straighten out the baby's eyes. Only when the child stopped eating and functioning did the mother decide to take him to the hospital. She was there, by the baby's bedside, when we arrived. Brian was there, too, making sure she stuck to the story that the baby had rolled off the bed. It was a story the medical personnel found utterly ridiculous—as did I.

We put the mother, "Tracy," in a room while we interviewed Brian in another. Going over and over his story again, he began to trip himself up, having to backtrack and remember what he'd told us in the beginning. It was all lies, and we knew it, but watching him squirm uncomfortably was something we enjoyed at the moment. When we were finished with him, we interviewed Tracy. Keeping her head down and staring at the floor the entire time, she stuck to the same story Brian had. I was disgusted and told her she was lying. As we were leaving the room, I made a comment: "Don't hold your breath for any Mother of the Year awards." She broke down completely at that point and started sobbing, admitting that she had lied and Brian had hurt the baby. She claimed she'd had no other choice, that Brian had threatened to hurt her if she told the truth.

After I took her complete statement, we went back to get Brian and...voilà! He was gone. Sensing his mistress was in the other room spilling the beans, he'd decided to make a run for it. We weren't too concerned at that point because we knew he would be heading for home and we would have a couple of uniformed officers waiting there for him.

Brian was arrested, and we executed a search warrant at his home, confiscating everything from prescription drugs to medical supplies he had gotten to care for the injured baby. I'll never forget sitting across from him in jail when it was all said and done. Brian had agreed to speak with us, and Dave and I had gone to visit him. This monster who tortured animals, women, and babies broke down and bawled like a child when faced with a future of incarceration. He knew he could never go up against a "real man" and win, which was why he's always made himself feel powerful by abusing women, children, and animals. I admit that I took pleasure in watching him sob, knowing he feared having to face years in prison.

In the end, the prosecutor agreed to a plea bargain of only eight years, and this monster is out now, father to his children and roaming the streets. As for the baby, he survived, but his future is grim. I can't say that I felt justice was completely served in this case.

I don't believe our justice system is able to truly protect our children. People sometimes express more outrage over an abused animal than they do in the face of child abuse, and I find that indefensible. Our children are innocent and depend on us to survive and grow. Anyone who interferes with that should be dealt the most severe punishment. As members of the criminal justice system, it's up to us to uphold this trust.

CHAPTER 4

It's Not Hollywood—The Bodies Are Real

I WAS FIFTEEN YEARS old when I saw my first dead body, up close and personal, outside of an open casket funeral.

It was during a ride-along with my father, and we were answering a "dead body" call at a downtown motel. No details about manner of death; it could've been a homicide, a suicide, or an accidental. I felt myself tense up when my father told me where we were going. This wasn't going to be a photograph; this was the real thing, and I had no idea what to expect.

I walked into the hotel room with eyes half-closed in fear, barely peeking at its contents. When I could clearly see that I hadn't walked into a chamber of gore, I breathed a sigh of relief and opened my eyes. Lying on the bed was an elderly man who looked as if he were sleeping, except his arm was sticking straight up into the air. *This isn't so bad,* I thought, and walked with my father over to the bed. The coroner and his assistant were turning the man over, and when they did, a loud gaseous burp escaped from the man's mouth. I almost jumped through the ceiling, which caused everyone in the room to laugh out loud. And when the smell of the burp hit me, I gagged.

"I'm gonna wait out in the hallway," I told my father, holding my nose.

The elderly man had died of a heart attack while he slept. He was in full rigor mortis, so when he was turned slightly, the arm that had been stretched across his pillow remained that way. Even out in the hallway, I could hear them "breaking down" the body, meaning the coroner was cracking any bones in full rigor to get the body back into its normal position. It's a god-awful sound, and one that I never got used to. Even at the end of my career, I'd cringe whenever I heard it. Photographs don't tell you things like that, just as they don't tell you about odors.

It goes right back to the question I'd asked my dad as a child: "What does a dead body smell like?" His answer—"You can't describe it, it's like trying to describe a color"—pretty much nailed it. The smell of a dead body is as distinct as a fingerprint or DNA: It is *that* unique. You only need to experience the smell one time, and you'll never forget it—and you'll always know what it is.

Police officers tend to react differently to the smell of death; some can handle it and some can't. Unfortunately, I am one of those who can't handle it very well. I am a "smell" person, which is why I never became a nurse (even though my father begged me to). The thought of working day in and day out around all those smells—bodily functions, bedsores, blood—was too much for me. Of course, as a police officer I encountered these smells all the time! And frankly, the smell of death caused my body to react involuntarily—I would start to gag and dry-heave. Not a very pleasant prospect. Obviously, I had to figure out how to handle it to keep doing my job.

When my father was a major crimes detective investigating homicides, he always carried a pack of peanut M&M's. Instead of smearing Vicks VapoRub under his nostrils, he'd pop an M&M in his mouth. He said blowing the smell of peanuts up into his nose worked far better than the Vicks. I tried it once.

I decided to stay with the Vicks.

I always categorized death in three stages—immediate, medium, and raunchy. The immediate is self-explanatory: There is no odor. A medium is anywhere from four to forty-eight hours old, depending on the weather or environment (put a medium in the hot sun or by an electric heater and it can become a raunchy in a New York minute), and permeates a significant odor. And the raunchy is full-blown vomit time. I had learned to deal with the mediums by using nothing more than strong mint gum. But a raunchy...you guessed it: Vicks.

Excluding children, the visuals of a death scene never bothered me much, just the smells. Of course, as with everything, there are exceptions. And by the end of my career, the visuals had begun to affect me more than I'd expected.

Those "cool" crime scene photographs that I pored over as a child and teenager left out the raucous smells, the horrible sounds, the grief-stricken screams of surviving family members. Real crimes are nothing like those "cool" photos; they involve human beings, someone's mother, father, child, brother, or sister. Since becoming a police officer, I no longer find dead bodies thrilling.

THE HUMAN BODY goes through some extraordinary changes immediately upon death, and there are those who find these changes fascinating (although I believe they would feel differently were they to witness them in person). I believe it's safe to say that I have seen bodies in every stage of decomposition, ranging from just after death to three years postmortem. I have seen dead bodies whole, without trauma, like the elderly who die in their sleep, and I have witnessed death so traumatic that the bodies we searched for had to be put together piece by piece, like a puzzle.

I've had people ask me how I could possibly handle seeing things like that. My answer was, "I have to handle it—it's my job." But that doesn't mean I am not affected by it. If you're human, you're affected.

There were a few instances where, although affected, I was intrigued. Some experiences simply shatter the notions of medical science and humanity. Every cop has a story like this, one of those "believe it or not" tales. The one homicide that comes to my mind certainly intrigued everyone at the scene.

A local woman, Linda Singleton, had gone missing. A vagrant and sometime drug abuser, she was not someone people paid much attention to. However, she had been involved in a lesbian affair with a married woman at the time of her disappearance, and police reports had been filed regarding the husband's threats toward her. One of our detectives stayed on the case for three years until a break came. The man's son (trying to get out of a prison stint for burglary) gave up his father by showing us where he had buried the woman: in the backyard of someone completely unconnected with the case. Can you imagine? And in case you're wondering, yes, those unfortunate people moved shortly after that. I would have, too.

Obviously, most of us assumed that after three years there would be nothing but bones left. I stood and watched as the backhoe dug up its first pile of dirt and dumped it. Rolling down the pile of dirt was a tennis shoe with an ankle bone sticking right out of it. Horrified, the lead detective yelled for the backhoe operator to stop, fearing he'd tear right through the body or scatter bones everywhere. They dug manually from that point on, expecting to find bones here and there, but they found the entire body intact. Wrapped in a black leather trench coat, Singleton's body was almost preserved—mummified. There was still a lot of tissue on the body, and to our astonishment the dirt underneath was damp from body fluids still draining. There were maggots, of course, and there was the smell. After three years I thought there'd be no smell, but I was wrong. Even though we were outside, large industrial fans were brought in. We had "bug experts" on the scene and experts in forensics, who determined that two unusually cold winters had slowed the normal stages of decomposition.

A few city workers who had brought in lights, tents, and a generator clearly were not prepared for what they saw or smelled.

And when boxes of pizza the sheriff had ordered for us arrived and were stacked on a table next to the evidence table holding the ankle bone and a few other "floaters," the workers were further appalled to see us standing around munching pizza as we watched the crime lab technicians methodically brush dirt off the body. I guess, in retrospect, I can only say that I was so completely awed by the forensic aspect of the scene that I didn't give anything else much thought. And I was hungry.

The bottom line is that there's no movie, no special effects, no camera angle on this planet, that could ever truly emulate a crime scene like Singleton's. Sure, the tents could be set up and the characters put into place, but one aspect will always be missing: the actual life that was taken, the broken family left behind, the emotions of those involved, and the sounds and smells that can be found only in real life—not on a Hollywood set.

I'll admit, sometimes officers can have unexpectedly inappropriate reactions at death scenes, which I consider to be a kind of defense mechanism. For instance, whenever I get nervous or upset I immediately start laughing—or talking a mile a minute. I can't help it; I've always been that way. The next story is a prime example of how officers can react under stressful circumstances.

I can't remember how the call was dispatched, but it wasn't what we initially thought. I believe we were told it was a "man with a gun" call (highest priority) and that the 911 came from the wife. Driving to the call, we assumed it had to be some form of domestic violence, so the adrenaline was coursing through our veins.

Upon our arrival, we were met at the door by an elderly woman in her bra who appeared to be in shock. She could only point to the bedroom. Guns drawn, we slowly made our way to the bedroom door and took positions around it, yelling, "Police! Put the gun down and lie facedown on the floor!"

No response. One of the officers did a "quick peek" into the room, and I saw his face immediately relax before he holstered his gun. We followed him into the room, where an elderly man lay on the bed after blowing half his face off with the gun that was still in his hand. It was a suicide. I know it sounds horrible to say that we all breathed a sigh of relief, but we did. We were expecting a possible shoot-out with an armed man holed up in there.

We stood there as one of the officers reached over to take the gun out of the man's hand. Just as he was about to put his hand on it, the man gave an involuntary "flinch" that just about scared the officer into flying right through the ceiling. He jumped about five feet back with a look of horror on his face, trying to retrieve his gun. The rest of us "lost it" immediately. I began laughing so hard, I found myself crouched in a ball by the side of the bed with my hand over my mouth, trying not to pee in my pants. Another officer was bent over inside the closet with his hand over his mouth, trying to stifle his own outburst. It just happened to be one of those incidents where tensions were at an all-time high and our bodies needed a release. That release came in the form of laughter. And the harder we tried to quell it, the harder we laughed. Seeing the officer who had just had the life scared out of him standing there sweating and shaking like a leaf was simply too much. I started to crawl on my hands and knees toward the door in a state of hysterics.

Unfortunately, I ran right into the wife, who had come to see what all the noise was. Standing there with a blank look on her face, still in shock, she stared down at me. Luckily, I had been laughing so hard that my eyes were streaming with tears. I slyly grabbed my keys off my belt and put them into my hand before standing up.

"Oh, here they are, I must've dropped them," I said between gasps of breath. Then I put my hands over my face and pretended that I was sobbing. "Oh, ma'am, I am so sorry! I just lost my grandfather last week, and this brought back those memories. Come on out in the living room with me, I'm going to help you...."

"Is—is he dead?" She peered over my shoulder into the room.

"Yes, ma'am, I'm sorry, he is."

Immediately, her face filled with an expression of heart-wrenching grief. It's always been that way: Whenever I tell someone a loved one has died, it's as if I can see that person's soul sucked right out. My laughter was gone in a flash, just like that.

I helped the woman to sit on the couch and held her hand while she cried. Her husband had been sick for a very long time and couldn't take living anymore. He hated being a burden to his family and felt that killing himself would be easier on everyone. But the anguish he left behind...!

This is why I hate suicides. To me, it is a terribly selfish, even coldhearted, act. In my opinion, suicides fail to give enough consideration to the consequences of their action—the lifetime of grief and heartache they leave behind for their loved ones to endure.

Certainly we all enjoy the shoot-'em-up and bloody gore that action and horror movies provide, but keep in mind—in real life, it's not Hollywood.

CHAPTER 5

Buckle Up or Die

A MONG THE MANY crimes and deaths I've dealt with as a police officer, automobile accidents are the most senseless...and no one is immune.

Imagine driving your family to church one day, everyone smiling, laughing, and discussing where you would all like to eat brunch afterward. Your three-year-old is buckled up in his car seat, and your two other children are giggling in the backseat. As you look toward your spouse in the passenger seat, you think how lucky you are to have such a wonderful family. But before that thought can even begin to make its way out of your head, you are thrown forward with such force that you lose consciousness. When you awaken, you're in a hospital emergency room surrounded by several doctors, nurses, and clergy. Your entire family has been killed.

It can happen that quickly. No rhyme or reason to it, no culpability, and you're left to pick up the pieces of what remains of your life. You try to understand how the teenager who ran the stop sign doing over seventy-five miles per hour and hit your vehicle, caving in the side directly next to your children, couldn't have stopped in time.

That's just one scenario.

An auto accident could result from the careless actions of an elderly person, a drunk driver, a housewife leaning over to pick up the pacifier her baby threw from the backseat, a priest, a doctor, a lawyer, a schoolteacher late for class, a teenager texting on his or her cell phone, even a police officer.... Any one of these people—in fact, anyone with a driver's license—can take someone else's life while driving. And it's often so heartbreakingly senseless: The majority of automobile accidents can be prevented.

It was an auto vs. pedestrian fatality that ultimately altered my feelings about being a police officer...erased the drive, eagerness, and anticipation I had previously experienced whenever I rolled up on a gory car crash.

An attractive young woman in her early twenties got into an argument with her boyfriend. Deciding to take a breather, she grabbed her purse, walked out the front door, and started down the road. In less than a minute, a dump truck carrying several tons of gravel came barreling around the curve, hitting her head-on while doing over fifty miles per hour. Lights out, cancel Christmas—a life has ceased, just like that. She never knew what hit her.

I arrived almost immediately afterward and watched as another deputy was covering what was left of the young woman with a sheet. Unfortunately, several passing vehicles had slowed down as soon as the accident occurred, when her body lay in full view by the side of the road. I began to wonder what it must be like for a normal person driving down the road to see something like this. What happens to the thirty-something woman driving to the grocery store when she passes a sobbing man by the side of the road, bent over the mutilated figure of a dead woman he's just hit with his dump truck? What did each of these people passing by this accident scene take home with them? How many of them had nightmares for months or were so traumatized that they had to seek counseling? What about the dump truck driver? Would he ever recover? What about the mother and the sister of the dead woman, who had arrived at the scene and were screaming hysterically while being comforted by the police chaplain? What about the boyfriend she had just argued with only minutes before?

These thoughts had never occurred to me until that day, perhaps because this particular accident affected me in an unaccustomed way...as a human being. Fatal accidents affect many, many people—not just the ones directly involved.

Driving is a privilege, not a right—but it wasn't until I became a police officer that I actually understood this. God knows I didn't understand it when I was a teenager. Frankly, when I look back at my early years of driving, I realize I'm damn lucky to be alive. Mortality simply wasn't an issue for me (or for any of my friends) at that age, nor was the idea of killing someone else. Not only were we irresponsible behind the wheel, we were dangerous and downright ignorant. But years later, when

I tried to explain this to teenagers I pulled over for speeding, I got the ubiquitous rolling of the eyes. And could I really blame them? Hadn't I done the same thing? It's a scary cycle.

I never wore my seat belt when I was young; now I don't drive to the end of my driveway to retrieve my mail without wearing it. Yes, I know there are exceptions, stories of people who were killed because they were wearing their seat belts and those who were survived because they weren't wearing one.

A woman doing thirty-five miles per hour hits a phone pole wearing her seat belt: Her neck snaps and she's killed. A drunken college kid is doing seventy-five miles per hour down a main city street and hits a phone pole with such force that his pickup truck explodes into pieces; he wasn't wearing his seat belt, was able to pull himself through the driver's-side window, and walked away with just a few scratches.

So, yes, there are a few exceptions floating around, but for every story like these two, there are hundreds to prove that wearing a seat belt does save lives.

As I said at the beginning of this chapter, anyone can cause a vehicle accident. Unlike other types of crimes, accidents do not distinguish among race, gender, social class, or background. I think this is why fatal accidents seem to affect police officers so profoundly: They're not about a local gangbanger gunned down in a drug deal gone awry or a domestic-related shooting; they're about innocent people going about their business and losing their lives for no reason. And they can happen to anyone, even cops. In fact, cops are at a higher risk than anybody. We have to drive fast, in unusual and dangerous conditions, all the while looking out for the safety of the public and ourselves.

Yes, fatal car accidents are among the most awful calls a police officer has to respond to—especially when they involve children.

Perhaps the most emotional and disturbing call in my entire career was an accident involving a vehicle. Several years after the dump truck incident, I found myself running my ass off on a hot summer day, responding to calls. We had calls pending for hours; we were being called off scenes to respond to higher-priority calls, and every call required lights and sirens. Domestic violence, robberies, burglaries, sex offenses, assaults—we dealt with them all within one single eight-hour period. I couldn't wait until my shift was over and I could go home. Of course, I knew I'd be damn lucky to get home on time.

About halfway through my shift, the call came in.

A young mother and her six-year-old daughter decided to go to the library. They walked out of their home to their driveway and got inside the car. The mother got into the driver's seat and heard her daughter shut the back door, signaling she was in. They were ready to go.

The mother backed out of her driveway and started down the road, speeding up to the fifty-mile-per-hour speed limit. Almost instantly, she heard her car make a loud rattling noise. She slowed down a little, hoping it would quell the sound. Only when she glanced in her rearview mirror did she realize where the sound was coming from.

She saw her daughter's shoe shoot out from behind the car onto the roadway.

What had happened was that the child had not gotten into the car as the mother had thought when she'd heard the car door shut. In a hurry, the mother hadn't looked into the backseat to make sure her daughter was there. For some reason, the child had decided to walk around the back of the car and get in the other side. When she was directly behind the car, her mother backed over her.

The child had gotten caught up in the car's undercarriage. The mother had driven approximately three hundred yards at almost fifty miles an hour before she'd realized what had happened.

I was the second officer to arrive at the scene, and what I found was indescribable.

Once the mother had stopped the vehicle, the child became dislodged. After throwing the child into the car, the mother drove back to her residence to call 911. When I arrived the child was lying on the front porch, the backs of her legs and buttocks almost completely gone. Obviously, the mother was hysterical, screaming and virtually incoherent. To make an already horrific situation worse, the woman's eight-year-old son was also in the residence. Seeing his mother and sister in the condition they were in threw him into hysterics as well.

I can't remember ever feeling quite so helpless. The residence was in a rural area, so it would take an extra few minutes for the ambulance to arrive. What do you say to a woman who has accidentally run over her daughter and is leaning over her, watching her die? There was nothing we could do to help the child. Miraculously, the little girl was conscious, but she was clearly in excruciating pain. At the time, I had a daughter around the same age, and it was all I could do to keep from losing it while I stood watching, completely helpless. Those few minutes waiting for the ambulance felt like hours.

Once they arrived, the EMTs began to work on the child quickly. Their eyes told me the child wasn't going to survive. We later learned that she had a severed liver and a skull fracture. My sergeant pulled me to one side and told me to drive the mother and her son to the hospital in emergency status. It was best that she be there when her child was pronounced dead.

Driving like a bat out of hell to the hospital, I did my best to comfort the woman while trying to keep my eyes on the road. Glancing in the rearview mirror, I saw that her son had calmed down considerably. Sitting in the backseat of a police car doing eighty miles per hour with lights and sirens blaring seemed to do the trick. He actually had a huge smile on his face and mouthed, "This is cool!" several times. But the ride in the patrol car obviously didn't have the same effect on the mother.

When we arrived at the hospital, we learned that the Life Flight helicopter had been dispatched and would be there shortly to transport the child to Columbus Grant Medical Center. In the meantime, the trauma team was trying to get her stabilized for the flight, but the prognosis didn't look good. The mother, the father (who had arrived also), the son, and other family members were whisked away to a family lounge to await the news.

Then came another sergeant of mine, delivering an order

I knew was coming but that I absolutely dreaded. I actually remember the conversation word for word.

"You need to get a urine sample from the mother," he said.

"Are you out of your fucking mind?" was my response.

"I realize it's going to be difficult, but she has to be tested for drug and alcohol use, especially since it looks like this is going to be a fatal."

"All right, then, head on in there and you do it," I countered.

"She's a female, you are going to do it, and that's final." He turned and walked away.

I stood outside the door of the family waiting area, wondering how in the hell I was going to tell this woman that she needed to give a urine sample to prove that she had not just killed her child while under the influence. I could hear her sobbing through the door, but I was immediately saved. A relative, I think it was her brother, walked out just then. I motioned for him to come over to me and was as blunt as I could be.

"There are times when I absolutely hate my job, and this is one of them," I began to explain. "By protocol, and by law, whenever someone is involved in a near fatal or fatal accident, a urine sample needs to be obtained. I'm a mother with a daughter around the same age as your niece, and if that were me in there, I don't know that I would be able to deal with what I'm asking...but I have just been ordered to take a sample from your sister. I think it would probably be best if a family member explained to her what needs to be done. I will do this as quickly as possible and get her right back here. Again, and honestly, I really don't want to do this, but I have to. Please explain to her that this is simply a procedural matter and that we are absolutely not insinuating she was under the influence of any drug or alcohol," I said quietly and calmly.

In law enforcement, we were taught to never apologize for doing our job, but in this case I could not have cared less. I didn't write the laws, and although I understood the purpose of the urine sample, I didn't have to like it and I didn't have to be a bitch about it, either.

To my amazement, the woman was more than cooperative. I watched as her brother whispered in her ear while she looked at me and nodded. Of course, as I escorted her to the nearest restroom, urine cup in hand, I saw many of the nurses look at me as if I were the devil himself. They didn't understand. They saw the big bad female police officer further traumatizing an already traumatized mother.

It was a difficult situation entirely.

As soon as we finished, the mother was taken straight to her daughter's room. She was getting ready to be rolled out to the Life Flight helicopter, having been stabilized by the trauma team (that alone was a miracle). As the team quickly moved the child, the packed emergency room became unusually quiet, watching. I saw nurses who hadn't even treated the child stand with their arms crossed, tears running down their faces. I did what I usually did: I held my own and stood by stoically.

It took a lot for me to show emotion on duty. In fact, the sexual assault on the little boy when I was a rookie was the first and last time I remember breaking down—until now. Quickly and with purpose, I headed right for my car. My work here was finished. And I barely had the door closed before the dam broke. Since I didn't want anyone to see me, I reached across my passenger seat as though I were looking for something... and sobbed.

It was very short-lived, however.

Within seconds, the dispatcher radioed and sent me on emergency status to a domestic fight in progress. There was no time for emotion, no time for reflection. I was expected to erase the incident from memory, collect myself, and return to duty. Much later, I learned the hard way that everyone needs time to grieve, to let it all out. Otherwise these emotions build through the years like a powder keg ready to explode.

The little girl survived. Frankly, it was a miracle that she did—and a testament to faith among those who might be inclined to question the presence of God. I had planned to stop by and visit her when she returned home, but the craziness of life continued and I never did. I'm still a little disappointed in myself for that.

One would think that over the years of seeing injured, decapitated, and burned-up bodies, it would get easier.

But it never did.

CHAPTER 6

Let's Dance

To POLICE OFFICERS, the word *dance* carries a special meaning, one not generally used under normal circumstances: It means "to fight." A cop wears many hats, and one of them is that of a boxer...kind of. The well-known "fight or flight" response has long been held up as a standard in law enforcement by police officers looking to test their co-workers' reactions in the face of adversity. According to them, the ones who stay and fight are the real men, while those who choose flight are an embarrassment to the badge. This isn't necessarily true; many times, those who puff out their chests and support this theory do so because they have something to prove to the brotherhood.

There's a difference between brawn and brains, even among police officers. However, it took me a long time to learn that. In fact, when I was near the end of my career, I became all too aware of those who looked forward to their shift so that they could "crack someone's skull." There weren't many, maybe a handful, but these Rambo wannabes brought up other, more disturbing issues. By bragging constantly about their strength and needing to prove it to their co-workers as well as to the public, they betrayed a compelling need for acceptance as "he-men" within their work environment.

When I was first cut loose to patrol the streets alone, I knew that back in the locker room, one of the most vocal worries of my male counterparts was, could I fight? Even more so, would I? Having a timid, submissive female as their only source of backup frightened them—and rightly so. I had several occasions later on in my career where my only backup officer, male or female, gave me cause for concern. Not every cop can be counted on to come through for his or her partners; it's a cold, hard, disturbing fact.

Needless to say, for the first few days on my own I was almost desperate to get called to an incident that would call for me to put my hands on somebody. I knew I didn't have any fears about doing so, and I wanted to put the guys' minds at ease and be accepted. They had never worked with a female officer before, and they were concerned. I wasn't going to go looking for a fight, but I sure wasn't going to shy away from one, either. Finally, on the third night of being on my own, I got my wish—and then some.

It was bar closing time. All the other officers on the night shift were on the north side of the city handling other calls, while I was in the south to handle calls there. I remember being a little bummed, because I wanted to be where the action was. However, when the dispatcher radioed me about a bar fight, I got a little more than I bargained for.

It turned out to be a very large fight at a popular nightclub frequented by kids from the university in the city and by locals. Approximately thirty to forty people were involved, the dispatcher said.

As luck would have it, I looked to my right and saw that I was directly in front of the club. In fact, I could see bodies rolling around in the doorway. For a second, I debated about waiting for backup, which in retrospect I should have done. But this was my chance, and I decided to take it. A few bruises and broken bones would be worth the acceptance I had been so desperate for, I thought.

So I whipped my cruiser right up to the front door of the nightclub, took a deep breath, and ran through the front door.

The scene inside brought me to a dead halt, the bartender laughed as she told my sergeant that my jaw dropped to the floor and my eyes got as wide as beer cans. Still, she added that she was damn impressed by what I did. After stopping for mere seconds to scan the pile of grown men pummeling one another's faces and dodging the beer bottles being thrown, I grabbed the two men closest to me, each in a chokehold around the neck, and ran outside, dragging them as if they were two footballs. I dropped them in the parking lot, ran back inside, and grabbed two more.

People always tell stories of adrenaline rushes, and I can assure you, I definitely had one that night. The men were squirming and actually swinging at me, but I held tight. Still, I was a little worried about what I would do with the four men in the parking lot, who were now even more pissed off at having been dragged outside by their necks—by a woman. Fortunately, as I brought the second set of fighting drunks outside, a few sheriffs' deputies who had been nearby were just racing up, lights and sirens blaring.

It all worked out. The other officers pulled into the parking lot, and I envisioned numerous pats on the back and cries of, "Atta girl!"

That wasn't what I got.

Frankly, I was a little shocked when the shift sergeant jumped out of his cruiser and laid into me.

"What the hell's the matter with you? You don't run into a fucking bar fight alone! You *wait* for your backup!" he screamed for all the cops, bar patrons, and God Himself to hear.

I was mortified.

No backslapping there, that's for sure. Nonetheless, that sergeant came over to me later with a calmer demeanor and tried to explain that I shouldn't have to feel that I had something to prove. *Yeah, that's what you think,* I thought.

He told me what the bartender had said and gave me a wink before he drove off. Then that particular sergeant did me the greatest favor I could ever have asked for. He told the entire shift, word for word, what the bartender had told him—how well I had handled myself. After that, I was as good as gold. I had finally proven that I would show no fear and was physically up to the job.

I was actually asked to join a couple of them for "lunch" the next night.

I look back on that night from time to time. Now, I would

never do that and really could care less what anybody thinks about it—I see clearly how stupid it was, how dangerous. But if I had that night to do all over again, would I have responded the same way?

Yes.

Obviously, there were other incidents on a much larger scale than this one. In fact, the one that comes to mind happened at that same nightclub. It actually elicited a smirk from the presiding judge before he asked me, "What were you thinking?" during the criminal trial. His comment kind of irritated me, but after I explained what had transpired, he understood.

I think.

I blame the man who was my supervisor at the time for the entire incident. Lieutenant Ray Roberts, notorious for escalating already heated situations, had practically no people skills and about as much common sense as an empty garbage can.

IT WAS A WARM FALL, and the nightclub was having frequent problems with overcrowding the bar. The university students packed in by the hundreds, and we had already responded to several fight calls. After the last fight, Lieutenant Roberts in all of his wisdom decided to play fireman and call into code the number of occupants inside the bar. It was only half an hour before closing.

Instead of calling the fire department to quietly enter the establishment and issue the club owners a citation, Roberts promptly announced at the front of the club, "That's it, folks! We're shutting her down! Everybody out!"

All hell broke loose.

Now, instead of having a few pockets of fights inside the bar, there was a crowd of over three hundred drunks—very angry drunks—rushing the door and flooding the parking lot. Some of them had just paid the ridiculously high cover charge and had been in the club less than five minutes. The club managers refused to reimburse anyone since they couldn't tell who had been there long and who hadn't.

I was standing to the side of the front door, ushering screaming patrons to their vehicles, when I noticed approximately five to six fights involving other officers in the parking lot. Each officer was fighting about two to three subjects. The sheriff's department and state highway patrol were being called in for assistance while the parking lot became one big boxing ring. I started toward the fights to help the officers but was having a hard time making my way through the crowd of people—they were everywhere. At that moment, I saw a black male a few feet from me causing quite a disturbance. He was standing with his arms crossed and screaming, "I want my fucking money back! I ain't fucking leaving until I get my motherfucking money back!"

I was on a step above him (which was why he didn't look so big at the time) and told him to leave immediately. His response? "I ain't leaving till I get my fuckin' money back!" Knowing my other officers needed help, I decided I didn't want to get tied up in an arrest right then. I issued my stern and final warning:

"You've got exactly two seconds to leave or you're going to jail."

"One, two," he said. "Now, watcha gonna do about *that*, bitch?"

All I know is that when I grabbed his arm to take him to the nearest cruiser, it felt as though I were trying to tow a tank. I barely had a grip on him before I was thrown face first onto the pavement. I made the grave mistake of putting my knee down to break my fall, and it immediately began to swell up like a balloon. Before I could even realize what was happening, I was dragged by my uniform shirt across the parking lot, then picked up and rammed headfirst into the back of a police cruiser.

As the guy jumped on top of me, he pulled at my face and I thought he was going to rip it off. I was able to get my shit together and actually stood up with him on me, just enough to slam him to the ground. Unfortunately, he had hold of my shirt and pulled me back down with him. We didn't have Tasers back then, only pepper spray. I grabbed mine with a vengeance, determined to empty the entire can into his face. Can in hand and aiming at the guy's face, I pushed the button. Nothing. The liquid merely pumped out and ran down my hand. (It was the first of several times that my can of pepper spray malfunctioned.) I had on my black leather gloves, so at least I didn't burn my hand. The only problem was, the guy grabbed hold of my hand, realized after his began to burn that there was spray on my glove, and flung his hand around—throwing the pepper spray into my left eye and rendering it useless.

Now I was on my back fighting with this maniac, kicking at him with everything I had. To make matters worse, a crowd of drunks had formed a circle around us, watching and taunting. I pulled my flashlight out of the ring on my belt and began swinging relentlessly. Other than my pistol, I was fresh out of weapons. At one point, when he was near my face, I grabbed the back of his hair, held his face near mine, and wiped my glove—saturated with pepper spray—across his eyes. The crowd roared. I remember hearing people yell, "Hey! You can't do that, bitch!" Out of the corner of my eye, I saw a few of them take a step toward us. That's when I started to worry. I was getting tired, and I certainly couldn't handle anymore.

In a flash, as the guy was trying to bash the back of my head into the pavement, I saw two blue uniforms descend on him. Ah, a reprieve—the cavalry had arrived. I was so grateful, I could have hugged them. They pulled the guy off me, and I rolled to the side and tried to stand up.

But it wasn't over. The crowd was becoming more hostile, so I had to back them off using only one good eye. (The other was closed, saturated with pepper spray and running mascara. I was a sight to behold, no doubt.)

It wasn't until I turned around to jump back into the fight that I realized what I had been dealing with.

One of the officers who'd come to my rescue stood at a towering six feet seven and weighed about 250 pounds, and he was a black belt. The other officer was no small chicken, either. Both were on the ground, on the bad guy's back, and the bad guy was lifting them both up—doing a push-up! It took approximately five officers to quell this psychopath and carry him to a cruiser. He was in the backseat less than five minutes before he kicked out the rear window and actually bent the metal window frame. He was already half out of the cruiser before the officers got to him.

The night ended with a trip to the emergency room for me—one of several in my career. Actually, I had no broken bones, just a bump on my head and a badly scraped and swollen knee. I realized how lucky I was after all was said and done. The large black belt officer learned years later, after he'd retired, that this particular fight either caused or contributed greatly to a debilitating back injury.

It turned out the bad guy was a linebacker for the football team at the university; big surprise there.

He was charged with multiple crimes, including several counts of assaulting police officers—all felonies. His attorney took a demeaning attitude and made a great effort to humiliate me during the trial.

"Officer Dittrich, do you want to tell me what made you think you could physically handle my client?"

I was appalled (and pissed), but I didn't answer because I was sure the prosecutor would object. The judge was one of my favorites, but even he couldn't pass up the opportunity to hear my answer. He let his glasses slide down his nose and smiled as he peered over at me.

"Actually, I'd like to hear that," he said. "What were you thinking?"

With my face turning several shades of scarlet, I decided to be as blunt as possible.

"Frankly, Your Honor, I was doing my job. And to be honest,

the guy had a hoodie over his head, was a step beneath me, and didn't look *that* big." I shrugged.

"Duly noted," he said, still smiling. "Now move on, Counselor...."

The defense succeeded in making me look like the ass of the day, but his client was found guilty, kicked off the football team, and ultimately left college because of his prison sentence. Plus, he had to pay for a new uniform since mine was ruined from the fight. Justice served.

After all of that, Lieutenant Roberts began to interview the drunken thugs who had stood by and taunted me while I was getting my clock cleaned, to determine if I'd used excessive force by swinging my flashlight at the bad guy. I was livid. Needless to say, the administration put him in his place, but for years afterward, he was always looking for a way to jam me up—make my life extremely difficult.

The funny thing is, the entire fight that night probably lasted less than five minutes. And as odd as it sounds, I never felt scared. Not that night. I remember the first fight where I actually was terrified—it was with a sixteen-year-old kid.

We had a report of an unruly juvenile who had left his house and had probably been drinking. Again, as luck would have it, I was sitting in a parking lot when the call came out and noticed a white male fitting the description of the teen, walking down the street right in front of my car. It was about three o'clock in the morning.

I pulled my cruiser alongside him and parked it, but he just kept walking. At that point, I wasn't sure it was the right kid.

As I walked behind him, trying to catch up, I called out his name. When he stopped and turned around, I knew it was the right kid. He ignored my order to stop and pulled away when I tried to grab his arm.

Keep in mind, this "kid" was over six feet tall and probably pushing three hundred pounds. This time when I grabbed for him, I pulled out my pepper spray. I had succeeded only in pulling off the cap and managed an "Oh, shit..." before the kid turned and grabbed me with both hands. He picked me up off the ground and tossed me like a beanbag about five feet, practically into my cruiser. I scrambled to my feet and managed to scream out an "Officer in trouble!" call on my radio as the kid was barreling over to me. Moments later, as we were squaring off, I could hear the sirens in the distance, coming to my aid.

It turned out to be a hell of a fight. Out of the corner of my eye, I saw several civilian cars brake at the sight of a little-girl cop fighting with a "ginormous" individual along Main Street. One guy actually got out of his car and ran to my aid, but as the sirens grew louder and closer, he backed off. Smart move. No one wants to be mistakenly thought of as an accessory to an assault on an officer when the other officers arrive. That guy later told me he didn't feel like spending the next week in the hospital. Even so, the chief of police sent him an "honorable citizen" award for his impeccable witness statement and testimony in court regarding the incident.

That night, I learned that all the hours of defensive tactic training become worthless in the real world. I tried to block the kid's punches, I tried pressure points, I tried to knee him in his common peroneal (back of the leg), I tried everything I could think of. And in the end, what did I resort to? Your basic chick-fighting tactics. I jumped on his back and began to claw at his face—his eyes, specifically—and rip out his hair. Miraculously, he fell to the ground and I was able to get one handcuff on before the other officers arrived.

This particular fight was a long one. The other officers were far away, and I grew extremely tired. I didn't ever remember feeling so tired—and I was shaking. It could have been fear, or it could have been adrenaline; either way, it was a horrible experience. I called Rich afterward and told him how I couldn't stop shaking. Later (after I retired), he told me that this was one of those nights he found extremely difficult to take.

Protecting and defending yourself is part of the job, and although there were times after a fight where I thought, *That was kind of fun,* most weren't.

What many people don't realize is that being a female actually kept me out of a lot of physical altercations. People think that the bad guys will see a female officer and assume he (the bad guy) can fight his way out. I learned just the opposite. Not all so-called criminals think that way. They may commit other crimes, but they feel it's "unmanly" to attack a woman. In fact, I've used that to my advantage several times.

I remember once being called to a bar where a guy was drunk and causing quite a disturbance. I got there first, went in, and walked over to the guy's table. He stood up, towered over me, and looked as if he were about to knock my head off.

Smiling, I leaned over and whispered to him, "Look, I got

called here because you had a little too much to drink and they want you to leave. As you can see, I'm alone here, and you would have no problem kicking my ass. If you want to do that, fine. But you'll have an entire police force here within seconds, and you'll be looking at years in prison. And believe me, you don't want to be known in prison for beating up a girl. Not to mention these people will look at me from here on out as a wimp, and that's pretty embarrassing to me. It would certainly make me look good if you walked out of here with me—you can go home and sleep it off."

The guy actually broke out into a large smile, tipped back his cowboy hat, and said, "You got it, darlin'."

Pride, in my book, was essential but always took a backseat to my own safety. Fighting and protecting myself on duty wasn't something I looked forward to, but it was part of the job—and no matter what happened on my shift, I saw to it that I went home at night.

My husband and my kids thanked me for it.

CHAPTER 7

Domestic Bliss or Battery

DOMESTIC VIOLENCE CALLS are among the most dangerous a police officer can respond to. The deepest, darkest emotions are at play; whether it's a spouse, child, sibling, or parent, domestic disputes generally involve extreme violence. They're also blind to race, gender, social class, and ethnicity. I've arrested doctors, lawyers, high-powered businessmen, the unemployed, and the homeless.

Domestic violence does not apply only to women: I have been in homes where the wife has unleashed a verbal and/or physical tirade against her husband, who generally turns out to be the type of man who insists, "I would never hit a woman."

An admirable stance, but not when your wife is beating you over the head with a skillet. You don't need to break every bone in her body, but at least defend yourself. Even more astonishing in such cases is the fact that it's usually the wife—not the husband—who calls the police. And when we ultimately arrest her for domestic violence, it's often *against* the husband's wishes! These types of husbands don't want their wives arrested. First of all, when it comes to abusive relationships, men are no different from women in terms of need and co-dependency. Abused men are just as insecure from years of verbal abuse and would be too humiliated if it were known that their wife had been arrested for assaulting them. They believe it would make them look weak—or so society says.

I once engaged in a theoretical debate with someone over what law enforcement calls "domestics." The person posed this question: "If women were historically in the position of power in the household—as men are and always have been—do you think the number of domestics would be higher or lower?" My immediate response was, "Lower." The person posing the question (a man) disagreed. Citing reasons from hormones to a higher incidence of mental illness and depression, he insisted that in such a world, women would be beating their spouses just as much as men do now. At the time, I thought his ideas were ridiculous, but later I decided he might be on to something with what he called his "PMS punch" theory.

At any rate, there are three types of domestics. First is the generic domestic violence call, which I personally call "the Simpson domestic." (I'm pretty sure the label is self-explanatory.) These are the worst of the worst. Responding to this type of domestic is extremely dangerous to everyone—sometimes fatal. This is also the type of call where a police dispatcher or 911 operator has to be on the top of things.

I can't possibly convey the number of Simpson domestics I

have responded to where the dispatcher failed to get the information necessary to ensure my safety. For instance, many times weapons are involved, and that is a key piece of information. Does the suspect have a weapon? Has he or she been drinking or doing drugs? Where is the suspect in the house? Where are you in the house? Are there children in the home?

These may not sound like difficult questions to answer, but they're crucial, especially when adrenaline is running high. The correct responses can save lives. Conversely, rolling up blind on a Simpson domestic—that is, without any information whatsoever—can be a nightmare.

It was late, and I was taking a leisurely patrol through the nearest run-down trailer park, trying not to fall asleep. As I turned onto another lane, I noticed someone at the end running toward me. It was a woman wearing a white bathrobe with red polka dots. Then, as she got closer, I realized they weren't polka dots at all, but multiple stab wounds—and she was screaming. In a split second, I was wide awake, every nerve in my body electrified. Immediately, I called for backup units and an ambulance and tried to make out what the woman was saying.

All I could hear her say was, "Help my son! Help my son!"

I had no idea which trailer she had come from or where her son was, and it was next to impossible to get this information from her—all she could do was scream. Moreover, I was concerned that the person responsible for the stabbing was running around the park, and I had no idea who or what I was looking for. I had to get through to her that I couldn't help until she told me which trailer she was talking about.

She spat out the number just as the other units and ambulance arrived, and we still had no idea who the suspect was or *where* he was. We approached the front of the trailer cautiously, with guns drawn, looking for another possible victim. When we reached the porch, we all took a deep breath: The porch was covered in blood, as if someone had taken buckets of red paint and splashed it everywhere. The blood took on a trail that led down the steps and across the street.

We split up; a few officers went into the trailer to look for the suspect, while I went with the others to follow the trail of blood. When this woman kept screaming about her son, I assumed she was talking about a little boy. So I followed this bloodbath and, stomach churning, prepared myself for the worst.

What we found at the end of the blood trail was not a small child (thank God), but a grown man who literally had been cut almost in half. He was the woman's "son." He had been sliced open—kidney to kidney—and was lying on the back steps of an unknown trailer. Blood poured down the steps in a steady stream, reminding me of one of those twenty-dollar Japanese fountains you can pick up at your local Walmart. It's funny the things that flash through our minds in moments of extreme stress.

To my astonishment, the man was still alive. As we called the EMTs over to our location, I heard on my portable radio that the suspect had been found and was in custody. Since this was ultimately going to be my investigation, I headed toward the scene of the crime. When I walked inside the trailer and looked around, I couldn't believe what I saw. Not so much the extensive collection of knives, some bloody, that lay around the trailer—no, it was the suspect himself. The guy was in his fifties but looked to be in his nineties, was probably shorter than me, and weighed about 120 pounds. A total scumbag. I know this wasn't the most professional thing to say, but I said it anyway:

"You mean to tell me *that* fucking guy"—I pointed at him—"is responsible for all of *this*?" I stretched my arms out dramatically to scan the blood-soaked environment.

"Can you believe it?" said the arresting officer. "The son was twice his size. Hell, Barbie, *you'd* have cleaned his clock!"

"Unbelievable...." I shook my head at the entire scenario.

How naïve I was then. As I surveyed the scene, I made the mistake of assuming the woman or her son could have easily overpowered the knife-wielding maniac. Worse, I looked down upon the woman because she hadn't. As we began to piece together the events of the night, things became clearer.

The woman had been involved in a horrifically abusive relationship with this scumbag for a year. The man beat her down mentally and physically. It was her grown son who convinced her to leave, only he wasn't around when she finally made the fateful decision.

To sum it up, the man held the woman hostage for over twenty-four hours with his prized knife collection, raping her on and off throughout the day. At the end, his drinking and frustration built up, and he unloaded on the woman he supposedly loved. He had been stabbing her repeatedly (almost twenty times) when the son, unable to reach his mother by phone and concerned, arrived at the trailer. As he walked inside and saw his mother on the floor, bleeding and screaming, the man came up from behind him and sliced him open.

It was only through the sheer will to live, or adrenaline, that the mother was able to pull herself up and run out the front door. The suspect panicked at what he had done and ran to a back bedroom. While the mother was out seeking help (me), the son dragged himself across the street to the nearest trailer.

It was an absolute mess.

The man responsible will be thinking about his actions for years to come in prison. But the incident opened my eyes to my own prejudices. Honestly, I walked around for a while after that, thinking, *What the hell do you expect? You lie with a dirty, drunken hillbilly like that and you get what you pay for.* I really didn't have a lot of sympathy for the woman.

This, even after my own short experience in a violent marriage. When I married young and had my oldest daughter, I justified staying by telling myself, "As long as I can get through the Police Academy and support us, I can hold out a little longer." Fortunately, it got to a point where I decided that as long as my daughter had food and love, we'd be better off homeless: Nothing was worth being treated this way. So I left and filed for divorce shortly after. Perhaps my own experience made my attitude even harsher. If I'd been able to leave, why couldn't all women? In my mind, that made all of the ones who stayed weak. Definitely not true.

Most women didn't have the support of family, the financial security, and the child care that I had available to me. I wondered later, if I'd never had all those resources, would I still be in that horrific relationship? At the time, civil protection orders were rarely heard of, and domestic violence was a "he said/she said" call. Today, women are still unaware of the numerous financial and support programs available to guide them through their "evolution." So they stay, and many ultimately pay the price with their lives.

I once responded to a domestic call where the man was the spitting image of my ex-husband. The wife had nothing, and they shared a little girl. No job, no diploma, no training, no family, and no means of getting out. It was scary to me. I remember taking the wife to a back room and asking her lots of questions, some that made her look at me as if I were psychic. She wouldn't say a lot, but when I told her, "Aren't you sick of waking up at night and seeing him at the foot of your bed staring at you? Aren't you tired of putting a knife under your pillow in case he finally 'snaps' in the middle of the night?"

She looked at me in shock.

"How do you know that?" she asked me softly.

"Let's just say there are many women who are or were in the exact same position you are—it's my job to know," was my answer.

Although these women had different faces, names, lives, and circumstances, they all shared a common situation: living with an abuser. Sometimes it was very frustrating to me and other officers. *Why don't you just leave?* But to these women, it wasn't that easy. Their abuser was their sole means of child care, financial stability, and, honestly, their existence. It was almost as if these men sought out women whose lives lacked stability. Think Drew Peterson: His third and fourth (one missing, one dead) wives came from broken homes, and he appeared as their "savior," showering them with the gifts they never had, love they'd never known, and financial security they could only dream of. Once they had completely turned their lives over, there was no going back.

But to me, the "bogus" domestics are even worse.

Over the last decade (post–O. J. Simpson), domestic violence laws have changed considerably. In my state, police officers are now required by law to make a physical arrest in a domestic violence situation if there are visible injuries. If there aren't any visible injuries, the victim can file his or her own charge of domestic violence, which also requires a physical arrest by the police. If no arrest is made when claims of abuse are verbalized by either party, law enforcement must articulate the reasons in detail.

These laws were put on the books to protect men and women in abuse cases. Many times, we would respond to calls where the victim (usually the wife) had extensive facial injuries or signs of abuse. We would hear the old "I fell down, and I'm not pressing charges" mantra and be on our way. Once we were gone, another beating would commence. With the new laws, evidence would be gathered to prove who was responsible for the beating, an arrest would be made on the spot, and a protection order would be issued—whether the wife wanted the charges or not and without her testimony. Apparently, the laws were meant not only to protect the victim, but to place responsibility for the arrest on police—at least in the eyes of the accuser.

Unfortunately, as with everything else in this country, there are people who abuse laws intended to support actual victims. Find out your husband is having an affair? No worries; just call the cops and say he shoved you into the wall, sign the criminal affidavit, and he's hauled off to jail. That'll show him! This type of bogus call happened frequently—and even worse, many officers didn't want to take the time to "articulate in detail" why an arrest wasn't made; it was easier simply to make the arrest. Having to interrogate the wife, interview witnesses, and further the investigation to determine she was lying was too time-consuming.

I disagreed vehemently with this. In fact, I would deliberately take the investigation to the next level so that I could charge the "victim" with filing a false report. Of course, the disdain and public denouncement I received from women's groups and violence advocates was overwhelming.

On one of my weekly radio shows (after I had retired), one of our guests was a well-known attorney for a women's group at one of the Ivy League universities. She was throwing out phenomenal statistics of female domestic violence victims and citing "studies" here and "studies" there. I asked a simple question:

"Do those numbers include the false reports that were initially titled as domestic violence calls?"

She was horrified. "No, of course not!"

"Considering I personally responded to false domestic calls

several times per month, I would think that you would factor that into your 'numbers.'"

I thought I was pretty nice about it, but I was subsequently set upon by the advocate groups, who were appalled by my statement. It was ridiculous. What they didn't realize was that false domestic reports need to be handled sternly. Why? Because through the years, the criminal justice system hasn't handled domestic victims the way it should, and the cops have a bad attitude about it. And these bogus domestics are the reason. They are actually doing more damage to true Simpson domestic victims, who need all the help they can get.

I went to a domestic once where the woman had hand marks all over her throat. Her husband had "choked" her, she claimed. Something didn't feel right about the call, so I started checking around. Turns out a neighbor had been outside smoking a cigarette and had watched as the woman walked out onto the front porch, choked herself, and then went back inside. I started to question the woman about her statement again, but she would have no part of it.

"I have marks, I want charges filed, and you *have* to arrest him!" she screamed at me.

I repeated the neighbor's observations.

Finally, the woman confessed to creating the marks herself—because her husband had taken her credit card. I took her to jail.

Sounds harsh, I know, but imagine a police officer handling two bogus domestics just prior to a Simpson domestic. Do you believe the true victim will get the attention or help that she or he deserves? In a perfect world, police are supposed to treat every call with fresh eyes and a good attitude. Well, it's not a perfect world, and cops are human.

Finally, domestic violence does not occur just between spouses and lovers—that's a widespread misconception. Many homicides are a result of domestics between parents, children, brothers, and sisters. In my eyes, the worst fell upon a fellow police officer that was brutally murdered by his own brother, corrections officer. The event was horrifying to all of us, thinking that something like this only happened to other people. But, it is a shocking realization that domestic violence affects everyone. I wrote a blog on the events that occurred that night and have included it here:

I remember the night all too well. December 26, 2007, my husband, Richard, and I slept peacefully after a long, festive Christmas Day. We were glad to see the year coming to an end. I was still a deputy with the Richland County Sheriff's Office, and Rich was a Mansfield police officer. We had endured one of those dark years in our profession, the kind that law enforcement agencies throughout history ultimately face. Our departments had been plagued with officer-involved shootings and deaths, all of which were scrutinized by the media. It was a year most of us went to work on edge, wondering if "today was our day."

Last Christmas was a peaceful holiday—thoughts of work put aside, as our daughters were always first priority—and we looked upon 2008 with high hopes. However, if we were ever to imagine how this year would end, we wouldn't have believed it.

It was approximately five a.m. the day after Christmas when our phones began to ring—our house phone and both of our cell phones—repeatedly, which is never a good sign in a household with two police officers. Rich and I were awakened and alerted to the fact that something was wrong—very wrong.

Unable to reach the various numbers that showed on our phones, I began to become extremely concerned about my father. A Mansfield police lieutenant, my father supervised Rich on the night shift. Since Rich usually takes Christmas off to spend with the family, I was racking my brain trying to remember if my father was on his day off or not. Although it had seemed like several minutes, only seconds had passed when Rich opened his cell phone and read out loud a text that had just come in: "Mansfield police officer Brian Evans was just shot and killed by his brother."

Standing in our kitchen in shock, Rich continued to read that Brian's wife, Trina, had also been shot. I immediately fell apart. I had known the couple for a long time; their ten-year-old daughter, Tess, was a friend of my daughter's, and the text didn't reveal whether Trina was alive or not. The thought of this little girl losing both her parents was too much to handle at that moment. Rich, who had worked side by side with Brian nightly, was also overcome with grief. Regardless, the incessant phone ringing began again, and we began to learn the horrific events that had occurred, leaving two innocent people dead and two shot.

Late Christmas night, Brian, a few friends, and his brother, Larry—a corrections officer at a nearby prison—decided to take in a movie. For reasons that can be defined only as premeditated, Larry excused himself from the theater and walked out, leaving the rest of the men scratching their heads. Brian and Larry had a good relationship, so no one could figure out why he did this. Unbeknownst to the rest of us, Larry had taken Brian's truck from the movie theater and driven it home. Becoming concerned, Brian called Larry's wife, Carol, and asked her to pick him up and drive him to their home to find Larry. Brian also called Trina, who was with his sister, Kimberly, and told them to start looking for Larry—something was wrong.

As Brian and Carol drove to Larry's home, they were unaware that he had already ambushed and shot his neighbor, forty-four-year-old Robert Houseman, in the head—killing him instantly.

After spending an enjoyable Christmas with his parents and two young daughters, the well-liked and quiet Houseman was definitely in the wrong place at the wrong time. As he put his keys in his front door to enter, Larry Evans approached Houseman from the darkness, leaving his body to lie on the front porch of the duplex they shared.

Brian spotted the body immediately upon pulling into Larry's driveway. Clearly sensing the danger, Brian ordered Carol to leave the area for her own safety. Brian, a highly trained SWAT member, was also certified in the area of crisis intervention. Emerging from the darkness carrying a high-

powered assault rifle, Larry Evans gunned down his own brother in cold blood, then shot at his own wife, who was fleeing for her life.

Mansfield police chief Phil Messer summarized Brian's courage well:

> "The fact that this was his brother makes the events even more tragic; however, it cannot be disputed his act to intervene instead of leaving in the vehicle with Carol Evans clearly saved her life and demonstrated his commitment to our oath. Yes, there may be a few among us who would have confronted such a situation in the same manner as Brian—the everyday heroes we read about from time to time—but there are those we expect to respond: our police officers and firefighters, what we call our hometown heroes."

Brian's body lay several feet from Houseman's as Trina and Kimberly made their way to the home. Lying in wait, Larry opened fire on Trina and Kimberly as they pulled in, striking Trina in the right shoulder and Kimberly in the chest. Reacting instantly, Trina threw her car in reverse and sped away for safety. As she called for help, her main priority was getting a message to Brian—to warn him not to come to the house. Unfortunately, she was unaware that Brian had arrived first.

What followed was a standoff between Larry Evans and my fellow officers at the Richland County Sheriff's Department and Mansfield Police. Over thirty rounds from various weapons were fired at officers, weapons that—according to Carol Evans, who never reported the incident—were being stockpiled over the course of several days. Carol Evans, who now supports her husband, also has her sister, Debbie Spurlock, on her side.

"Larry's a good, good person. Everyone needs to know that," Spurlock stressed about the barbaric monster who had brutally killed two people and shot two others.

In no less than a cowardly fashion, Larry stripped off his clothes and surrendered to authorities, naked with his hands held high, knowing he wouldn't be shot. In the aftermath of the brutal slayings, Evans was indicted on nineteen counts of murder and attempted murder of Brian Evans, Robert Houseman, Trina Evans, Kimberly Evans, and countless law enforcement officers. His bond was set at $1 million. Prosecutors, at that time, were seeking the death penalty.

The trial of Larry Evans began—and ended—this week. Trina Evans courageously filed a motion to continue the trial, contending the findings of the psychiatrists were grossly inaccurate; the motion was denied.

This is only part one of an incredibly tragic story that has taken an astonishing turn of events. With the insanity plea thrown into the mix, the trial has already sparked outrage within the community, and numerous protests have already begun in downtown Mansfield. Was Larry Evans completely under the influence of a psychotic breakdown, or were the killings calculated by an intelligent, cold-blooded killer who knows the inner workings of the criminal justice system?

There is a growing and all-too-realistic fear that Larry Evans may be out on our streets one day soon. While incarcerated, Larry has sworn to finish the job he started—a job that includes killing Trina and Kimberly.

On Tuesday, September 2, a three-judge panel (two, actually, since the third fell asleep) deliberated for only ten minutes after listening to the testimony of only one witness, a psychiatrist for the defense. The judges returned an appalling, and shocking, verdict of not guilty by reason of insanity. A potential mass murderer may be on our streets in less than two years, as Larry Evans attempted to shoot and kill upward of fifteen people that night. At the announcement of the verdict, the courtroom erupted, stunning the victims, including Trina Evans.

As for Trina and Tess Evans, they are slowly picking up the pieces and holding their breaths.

Domestic violence is serious, and the effects of it will continue to ripple through society and the lives of innocent people for years to come.

CHAPTER 8

A Sexual Predator Is Lurking

L IKE MOST DECENT people, I am repulsed at the thought of child sexual molestation. Most violent crimes make us shudder, but molesting an innocent child for personal gratification is in a class by itself, at least in my opinion. As cops, each of us tends to focus on a particular crime or criminal behavior, gaining expertise in that area or choosing to view it as more heinous than the others. Clearly, my trigger happens to be the child sexual predator.

I cannot fathom why someone would want to traumatize, terrorize, and do violent physical injury to an innocent child—a baby. What drives a grown man to violently rape a six-month-old baby, sometimes to the point of death? If a grown man is that sexually frustrated and wants to terrorize someone, why pick on a baby or a five-year-old girl?

Why do these men, and sometimes women, find their sexual gratification not just by having sex, but by having sex with a child? Most don't want to be branded a baby rapist or baby killer, so one would assume that if grabbing the nearest hooker would suppress their urges, they'd do it. But it's the idea of the young, the body of a child, the innocence that surrounds them, that turns such people on.

I'm no psychiatrist, but I've been around enough of these animals to see what makes them tick. And I get angry when I hear some psychiatrists on the witness stand—after no more than one or two encounters with the subject—say, under oath, "I believe in my professional opinion that with the right amount of counseling and medication, the defendant will be able to lead a life free from the victimization of children." Some of these doctors don't have a clue, but they're paid well for their testimony.

Even worse is when these experts come out with "statistics" on recidivism for child sexual predators. The Department of Justice cites recidivism rates as low as 3 percent—then goes on to say that a sexual predator is four times more likely to commit another sex offense than another non–sex offense felon! There are people who object to "Megan's law" and others like it, arguing that they were put on the books based on recidivism "theories," not on facts. I cannot understand such people, who publicly challenge laws that are there solely to protect children. I wonder if they would be so vocal if their own child became a victim.

I've come up with my own profile of child sexual predators, free of all the legal jargon and psychiatric bunk. To me, it's pretty simple: No one can force another human being to change or control where sexual attraction is directed. Period. If our justice system could accept this, the laws and sentencing of child sexual predators would become much easier, and these monsters would never be allowed back on the street again.

Go up to a heterosexual male and tell him, "Starting tomorrow, you will live your life as a homosexual. Period." The man would most likely recoil and convulse at the thought. Do the same, reversed: find a homosexual male and tell him, "Starting tomorrow you will live your life as a heterosexual. Period." The same reaction will follow. Now, find a pedophile. "Starting tomorrow, you will live your life as a hetero- or homosexual male. You will only have sexual contact with adults. Period." That notion to a pedophile is horrifying. They *can't* change. No one can force another human being, or control where their sexual attraction is directed at. It's who they are and, accepting this fact, the laws and sentencing of child sexual predators would become much easier.

Quite frankly, I find these people *almost* as sickening as the predators themselves. Here's what I believe some of these "statistics" don't take into consideration. Child sexual predators are *not* ignorant people. In fact, most of them are quite educated. If a predator is caught, convicted of, and punished for downloading child pornography on the Internet, do you really believe he'll take the chance of doing it again? No, he'll simply find other ways to achieve the same sexual gratification.

Whether it is unassumingly taking photographs of neighborhood children or renting a post office box for receiving overseas pornography, the predator is *still* offending. This time, he's not getting caught. Does anyone truly believe that a man with such ingrained behavior just stops, all of a sudden?

Here's a story sure to alert parents everywhere and a prime example of the lengths sex offenders go to in order to avoid getting caught. If you've read my fiction book *The Devil's Closet,* the story is sure to sound familiar.

I was working in the detective bureau when I was contacted by the FBI in reference to a "questionable" photograph that was downloaded by a man who lived in my jurisdiction. The photograph wasn't exactly sordid; it was of a young girl, around five years old, posed in a ballerina costume. It might not have alerted anyone else, but in law enforcement such things this tend to raise red flags.

We did a brief criminal history check of the man—whom I'll call Edward Barnes—and it turned up zilch. Edward was in his mid-fifties, lived with his grown son, had worked at the same factory for over twenty-five years, and had never even had so much as a speeding ticket. When the FBI agent, Paul, accompanied me and another detective, Jim, to the factory where the man worked, we weren't expecting much. *Probably has a granddaughter who likes ballet or something, no biggie,* I thought.

Needless to say, we were in a room with Edward for less than five minutes when I realized that something was "off" with him. He was extremely nervous, very introverted, and refused to make eye contact with me. He told us that he'd ordered the ballerina picture because he'd thought it was "pretty."

We were seated at a table with Edward as Paul was asking him standard questions. Now, I had always found, when dealing with someone like Edward, that if you take them off guard, you'll get the most truthful answers. So as Paul's questions droned on, I blatantly interrupted with my own.

"Edward, why don't you tell me exactly what age range of little girls you are sexually attracted to?"

"Between five and eleven years old," he said matter-of-factly, staring down at the table.

We were stunned, now alerted to the fact that we were dealing with something much bigger. We asked him if there were more photographs at his home similar to the ballerina. Yes. Was there anything inside his home that we would find concerning? No. Could we take a look inside his home with him present? Yes, but not my bedroom.

Uh-oh.

We drove behind Edward en route to his residence and noticed he was using his cell phone. When we arrived at his home and followed him up onto the porch, we were astonished to see an entire computer smashed to pieces sitting right there.

Next to it was a large black garbage bag. I was pretty angry at that point. Knowing Edward had called his grown son from the car and ordered him to destroy evidence incensed us all. Of course, we had no idea what we were in for when we stepped inside the house.

Unfortunately for Edward, Jim was on the phone with one of the detectives back at the police department, telling him to get us a search warrant. Edward's admission, the photograph, and the smashed computer pretty much justifed a warrant, and we were confident we would find more inside the house. But we really wanted to get into his bedroom.

Edward's hand was shaking as he opened the front door. Jim and I gave each other knowing glances as we walked inside. We were met by Edward's grown son, Nathan, who was trembling and seemed just as nervous as his father. Looking around the family room and kitchen, we didn't see much to raise concern: a little marijuana, dirty dishes, and an over-flowing garbage can. Paul asked Edward to get the other photographs that he'd admitted having. Edward walked into the living room and handed Paul a photo album.

When Paul opened the album, my stomach convulsed. These weren't pictures of little ballerinas; some of these photographs were appalling: small naked children in graphic sexual poses. Probably what stunned me even more than the photographs was the fact that Edward had so nonchalantly handed us the album—knowing its contents. It appeared that he didn't think there was anything wrong with them. If that was the case, I couldn't begin to imagine the horrors on the computer that had gotten smashed!

Paul looked at him, astonished. "Uh, Edward, you told us at your job that these photos weren't that bad."

Edward merely shrugged, looking uncomfortable.

"Can we look in your bedroom, Edward?" I started toward his bedroom door, which was just off the kitchen.

He stepped in front of me. "No! I told you no, you don't have my permission!"

"Okay, that's fine," I said calmly, and noticed a staircase.

"Can we go upstairs?"

"I...I suppose." By now, he was sweating profusely.

Basically, we needed to stall as long as possible, to give the department time to get the warrant completed and signed. Jim had already called the detective writing the warrant to get him to add the information on the photo album.

Searches are tricky. Yes, Edward had given us consent to search certain areas, and we'd found more than enough for probable cause, but only in the general area in which the contraband was found—not in the bedroom. We clearly had enough to arrest Edward for child pornography, but a search warrant would make the evidence and arrest airtight. And it would give us free rein to search the rest of the house, including the bedroom. Luckily for us, it was the middle of the day, so the judge was in his chambers, ready to review and sign the warrant.

When I got upstairs, I found more startling photos. This wasn't mail-order kiddie porn. By the upstairs window, lying next to a camera, were photographs of little girls playing in sprinklers wearing bathing suits, little girls playing hopscotch and riding their bikes on the sidewalk. In the corner of each photograph was the distinct image of a window frame.

I looked out the window and back at the photographs, realizing that Edward stood at that particular window taking photographs of little girls in the neighborhood. As a mother, the thought horrified me. Little did the parents in that neighborhood know that their daughters were being photographed for a grown man's sexual gratification.

There were other, equally horrific photos in the pile. Apparently, Edward liked to frequent pee-wee football games. There were numerous photos of the pee-wee cheerleaders—and not just their faces, either. When the cheerleaders gave a vivacious kick to cheer on their footballers, Edward snapped a picture of their vaginal areas. I'm sure to parents sitting around him, he was just another parent taking pictures of his proud son or daughter. This man was sick, but at that point I still hadn't realized just how sick.

A short time after that, the other detective arrived with the search warrant. When we served it on Edward and informed him we would be going into his bedroom, his face paled. I was almost hesitant when opening the bedroom door; I had visions of body parts, photos of child graves, and whatever else my overactive imagination could come up with. Still, I wasn't prepared.

Edward's walls were covered with magazine pictures of child movie stars, JCPenney child catalog pictures, and other child advertisements. There were pictures of Shirley Temple, the figure-skating champion Oksana Baiul, Drew Barrymore, and numerous others. They covered the wall completely—all little girls. Standing upright next to Edward's bed was the most grotesque doll I had ever seen. It was life-size, approximately three feet tall. He had put a long black wig and dark makeup on it, added a black dress and black boots, and painted its fingernails black—it was a "goth" doll. On the dresser was a full-blown *Bride of Chucky* doll, from the famed horror movie series. Lining the wall bookcases were numerous children's books ranging from *Alice's Adventures in Wonderland* to *The Wonderful Wizard of Oz*. Frankly, the room was so disturbing that anyone under the age of thirteen would have had nightmares about it. In his bathroom was a menagerie of women's makeup—and silicone breasts. As we stood, silent and gasping, the detective who'd brought the search warrant, Dave, tried to make a jovial crack.

"It puts the lotion in the basket and rubs it on his skin," he said with a deep voice, mimicking a line from the movie *The Silence of the Lambs*.

This guy made the serial killer Buffalo Bill in that movie seem almost normal. But Dave's "joke" seemed to resonate with all of us, because he wasn't far off the mark. Noticing the closet doors, I decided to start with them. Several years and many a nightmare later, I wished I hadn't.

I pulled open the two closet doors simultaneously. Standing before me were approximately three rows of the life-size dolls, all dressed in high-end clothing and wearing expensive shoes. There were rows and rows of expensive children's clothes and dressers full of little-girl underwear, socks, and books. Some of the underwear had brown stains on them.

"Get out of here!" was my only response. Was this actually possible?

The other investigators came over, saw the closet's contents, and made their own statements on the matter. Edward, who was standing outside the door with a uniformed officer, said nothing. We all knew at that point what the dolls were for. I went over to the goth doll that sat by his bed and picked it up. When I felt certain "items" underneath its dress, I cringed. After pulling up the dress, I saw that Edward had attached small plastic breasts—nipples and all—to the doll. I shuddered to think what was under the underwear but had to look anyway. In the vaginal area, Edward had glued a sponge that had been cut into a triangle shape and slit it down the middle. Then he cut up hair netting and glued it onto the sponge to give the appearance of pubic hair. I was sick to my stomach, knowing what he was using the doll for.

"Oh, Jesus Christ!" Jim cried after seeing the doll's "genitalia." "What the fuck is that shit, Edward?"

"I just don't want to hurt any little girls," Edward said quietly.

Disgusted, I grabbed a garbage bag to put the doll into. I had every intention of introducing it as evidence. Watching me, Edward flipped out.

"What—what are you doing? You can't take her...*please*!"

He was genuinely upset, grief-stricken. Even when we found videos that had been shipped from Mexico of little girls acting provocatively and other evidence to use against him, all Edward cared about was his favorite doll.

The FBI took the smashed computer in an attempt to recover the information from the hard drive, Edward was booked on charges of possessing child pornography (a felony), and we took him in for questioning.

His interview was sickening.

Basically, Edward had always had an affection for children. It started out years before with a few peeks here and there at children playing outside. Then he progressed to getting child porn via mail, and when the Internet came on the scene— Eureka! Distraught by his urges, Edward felt the only way to satisfy them was to use the dolls. He wasn't hurting anyone, or so he told us.

This was a man who by his own admission had thought about little girls sexually twenty-four hours a day, seven days a week, for over two decades. We could see how his actions progressed, so to believe that he had never actually touched a child was pretty naïve. We had uncovered evidence that he traveled frequently, so God knew what he did when he was away.

When his elderly parents posted his bond, things became even more unusual. Over the course of the weekend, Edward left over sixty voice mail messages in my office, demanding his doll back. Since we had already taken numerous photographs, the county prosecutor suggested we return it. The day Jim and I pulled into Edward's driveway to return his doll will never be forgotten.

We had called ahead to let him know we were coming. Before our car was even in park, Edward came blasting out of his front door at a dead run. He looked as though he hadn't slept in days; he was pale, sweating, and shaking. I purposely took my time retrieving the thing from the trunk while he stood there, wringing his hands. He grabbed the doll from my hands, fell to his knees, and hugged it with such emotion that Jim and I were speechless. This man had not been able to sleep, eat, or function for two days while his favorite doll was gone. It was one of the most disturbing things I had ever seen.

Two days later, we received a call from Edward's son that he was gone and had left a suicide note. The note basically said he wasn't going to put his family through the anguish and he would rather die. He was found within a day and taken to the state psychiatric hospital.

Things quieted down a little after that; we all put hours of work into the case, only to hit a wall in the form of the county prosecutor and our own department. Edward had passed a voice stress analysis test in which he was asked if he had ever touched a child. Apparently, that was good enough for everyone. I was pretty livid over the matter. Later in my career, I became an operator of the voice stress analysis test, and I can assure you that mistakes get made, results can be read improperly, or people can simply pass it, period. Because of this, the stains on the underwear were never tested and no further questioning or investigation took place. Translation? *We don't want to spend the money.*

Nice.

Several months later, I was sitting at home on my front porch when I received a disturbing phone call. It was a police dispatcher from my department. She told me that the forensic center that was evaluating Edward had called. They had explained that by law, they had to make a "duty to warn" phone call if they felt someone's life might be endangered by a client they were treating. That someone was me, and the client was Edward.

I called the doctor, who literally had Edward in the next room for a session. The doctor told me that Edward suffered from schizophrenic affective disorder and had made legitimate homicidal threats toward me and my family. "Credible" threats, according to the doctor; he said he truly believed the minute Edward left his office, my family and I would be in imminent danger.

Fabulous. I called the county prosecutor, who immediately revoked Edward's bond on charges of aggravated menacing (threatening a police officer), and he was thrown back in jail.

In the end, Edward was sentenced to serve ten months in prison for child pornography and aggravated menacing. There was no law on the books that said someone couldn't have sexual relations with inanimate objects, and there was no proof that he had violated any children. Since this was before Ohio had passed Senate Bill 10, Edward didn't even have to register as a sex offender upon his release. Of course, it was my understanding that Edward was going to be shipped to the state psychiatric hospital immediately upon his release from prison, but the county mental health facility never filed the paperwork. Throughout Edward's brief stint in prison, I received a handful of phone calls from prison officials and corrections officers who had overheard conversations and intercepted letters Edward had written to me. They ranged from threatening to slit my throat to vowing to kill my family.

Edward is a free citizen now, out roaming among our innocent children with no one watching him. Do you think he's dangerous? I certainly do. What's even more frightening is that this is one man in one small town. Imagine how many more of them exist across this country.

So to all those defenders of the violators of children, I hope you take this story into consideration next time you stand hand in hand with a child sexual predator.

CHAPTER 9

Badge Bunnies

A LSO KNOWN AS "cop groupies," "gun suckers," and "badge chasers," bunnies have been a part of law enforcement from the beginning. And their numbers are many. My own quote, "Marriages in law enforcement make Hollywood marriages look like the Bible belt," evolved directly from my experiences with badge bunnies. Any woman married to a police officer needs to be made of some pretty stern stuff. Not to say that every cop cheats—a lot of them don't—but some of the come-ons and body parts exposed their way would make Angelina Jolie insecure.

Looks don't matter to badge bunnies—it's all about the uniform and the power. I've seen the most unattractive and overweight cops get sexual propositions from bunnies. Frankly, I feel a few officers out there became cops for this reason. They were loners, nerds, bullied in school, and never had girlfriends. Once they put on the uniform, they had power, and suddenly women were chasing them.

If you think of a badge bunny as a young, slutty-looking girl standing on a street corner, you're wrong. Well, there are some like that, of course, but bunnies come in all flavors: They are nurses, police dispatchers, convenience store clerks, corrections officers, secretaries, bartenders, waitresses, and (ahem) female police officers, to name a few. Just as some officers become cops to attract the bunnies, some bunnies obtain jobs solely because they offer frequent contact with law enforcement.

And it's not just male officers who get approached by bunnies, though they certainly get the lion's share of attention. I've been propositioned while on duty—by men and women both. Lots of officers lose their marriages because of a bunny, but I've known a few who lost their marriages, their jobs, and their freedom. That's right, they went to prison. Imagine a cop getting dumped for a bunny by another cop; he gets pissed, breaks into her house to see what she's up to, and voilà! He gets himself fired and tossed into the slammer on a burglary charge.

The fact that an officer is married is irrelevant to a bunny. In fact, she sees this as even more of a challenge, which makes it even more appealing. The secrecy of it and the cat-and-mouse games are turn-ons for both the bunny and the officer. I worked with an officer once who obtained four phone numbers with invitations attached in one eight-hour shift. "Here's my phone number and address, my front door will be unlocked so come find me when you get off work!" many of them read. This was not unusual, by any means. And a few officers didn't want to wait until their shift was over, so they'd get a blow job right there in their cruiser. Or they'd take their "lunch break" at a bunny's house for a quick sex romp.

Bunnies who become female police officers are probably the most "powerful" of them all. Not every female officer belongs in this category, only a small percentage. Usually, they'll start out in a subordinate position within the department—a dispatcher, a meter maid, a corrections officer, a caseworker. Then, once they get through the Police Academy (usually sleeping with instructors along the way), they are sworn in and it becomes a free-for-all. These women usually perform below average as officers, and many of *them* are married to non-officers. For the first couple of years on the job, they sleep with as many of the officers as they can, starting with their training officer. Once they've made their way around the department, they count on these officers to carry them on the job. They expect the officers to take their reports, answer their calls for service, and jump to attention at the snap of their fingers. These women get promotions easily and climb the ladder of success while lying on their backs. If they're lucky, they'll find officers who will leave their wives for them, but it usually doesn't last. Around the ten-year mark, most officers have their eyes opened to these women, who are subsequently considered "damaged goods" for the rest of their career and are pretty much shunned.

As for the female officers who don't fall into the bunny category, they can zero in on one who *is* faster than you can say "catfight." Legitimate female officers absolutely loathe bunnies. I always found that the more the bunny cop was chastised, the more the guys tried to "protect" her—for a while. I had my own experience with a bunny officer I worked with, Lolita, and I learned it's best just to play nice and let nature take its course.

Let me be honest: Whenever a bunny cop was hired at my husband's department, I worried. Sure, we've got an awesome marriage and I trust him completely, but I am also realistic. If I were to believe that any human male didn't find an attractive female cop tempting, that would make me pretty naïve, walking around with my head in the clouds. That's not me. Rich, on the other hand, was fully aware that I was hit on periodically by fellow officers, and it never seemed to bother him—he trusts me. I think it's different for women. Most, not all, women stay faithful; that's the way history has played out. Men, however, can have the best of intentions, but stuff happens and they screw up.

My own parents' marriage didn't survive the bunny population; neither did the marriages of two of my uncles. An overwhelming majority of my cop friends have been to hell and back because of their indiscretions with bunnies. That's why growing up—and when I entered law enforcement—I swore I would never be married to a cop. Of course I am now, and I was actually accused by a choice few of being a bunny.

It wasn't because I started off as a police dispatcher before becoming a female officer. Everyone knew my family, so they understood that I was merely following in my father's footsteps. When Lolita and I were the first two female officers hired at the Mayberry Police Department, I knew what most people were expecting—that we would be bunnies. I took a personal oath that I would never engage in a relationship with anyone within my department. I'm proud to say I stuck with that, but it's likely that staying on my feet instead of my back actually kept me from advancing. And that was fine with me—at least I knew I had truly worked for my achievements.

Nonetheless, on my first year on the job I was still reeling from a disastrous first marriage, working lots of hours, taking care of a baby, and doing my best to be accepted at the department. At that time, Rich was a patrol sergeant with the county sheriff's department and worked the same shift I did—nights. I had a routine of stopping at the same gas station every night to grab a coffee. The first time I ever met Rich, I couldn't stand him.

I was walking out of the gas station, and he was coming in. I had heard stories about Rich Dittrich. He was on the SWAT team, was a former national judo champ and current third-degree black belt, was a good-looking ladies' man, and had some big "guns" (arms) that aided in his "beating the living shit" out of those who truly deserved it. Some of the guys would say, "You don't want to fuck with Dittrich." I heard the stories in passing and never paid much attention. To me, they were just a bunch of testosterone-fueled conversations about who was the bigger bad-ass.

That night, I had an overwhelming craving for caramel popcorn, so I had a box of Crunch 'n Munch in my hand along with my coffee. I didn't know many of the sheriff's deputies since I was a new city cop, so I thought I'd start a conversation. It didn't go so well.

"Hi there! How are you?" I asked cheerfully.

He eyed the box of Crunch 'n Munch and smiled. "You know that shit'll make you fat, sweetie."

He kept walking into the store while I stood there with my face turning five different shades of red in embarrassment. By the time I got into my cruiser, I was livid. I needed to vent, so I radioed one of my fellow officers on the shift to meet me in a nearby parking lot. (Cell phones hadn't exploded on the scene yet.)

"I just met Sergeant Dittrich," I said angrily when he arrived.

"Oh yeah? How's Richie doin'?" the officer said, and then noticed my face. "What happened?"

"That is the most arrogant, conceited asshole I have ever met in my life! Oh, my God! I cannot believe you all like that guy!" I told him what happened.

The officer began laughing out loud, which further incensed me, but then he tried to offer an explanation.

"You gotta know Rich, he was just fucking with you—that's how he is."

"I think he's a serious asshole."

I drove around for the next two hours, still upset about the incident.

Today, when Rich tells the story, it comes out differently. He says that prior to the gas station controversy, we had passed each other in the city in our respective cruisers. Both times, he said, he waved at me while I looked straight ahead and kept on driving. So he thought I was a snob and was giving it right back to me. It is a charge I vehemently deny.

The next run-in I had with him, I was sitting in a parking lot doing paperwork. He was just coming into the city and saw me, so he pulled up alongside me. I saw the cruiser pull up and expected it to be one of my own guys. When I looked up and saw it was a sheriff's car with Rich at the wheel, I kept my window rolled up and went back to my paperwork. To get my attention, he shone his flashlight in my face, which prompted me to roll down my window angrily.

"Get that light out of my face, I'm busy."

He smiled. "Aw, c'mon, you're not still mad, are you? I was just messing around...."

He was persistent, I'll give him that. It took a while, but I began to see that he really wasn't so bad. In fact, he was quite nice. From then on, we spent many nights side by side in our cruisers, talking for hours. Night shift in wintertime can be horribly boring, so it was good to be able to pass the time. I never looked at Rich as anything more than a friend at that time.

Why?

Because Rich was married.

I had watched my family marry an average of three times each, and I had been cheated on constantly by my ex-husband. So I swore I would never be one of "those" women. I was going to live my life honorably, no matter what it took. And it worked...for a while. I never even allowed myself to consider Rich as more than a friend. Then, about a year after we met, he transferred to the Mansfield Police Department—my father's department. We kept in touch and talked frequently. I even casually dated another officer from that same department for a brief time. I was living in Mansfield at the time and making the twenty-minute drive to nearby Mayberry, then working the afternoon shift. Rich and I had something of a routine going on. He worked the night shift in Mansfield and started at ten p.m. My shift ended at eleven p.m., and several times a week I would meet him in a parking lot near my house after work. We'd chat about the day's events or calls that we'd handled—cop talk. A lot of times he'd get called away since he was working, and we'd talk for only five minutes. No big deal.

I don't know how or why, but on one particular night I met Rich as always after work. He got called away after a few minutes, and I went home. For some reason, that night I felt differently. I remember walking through my door thinking, *I miss him. What the hell is going on?* Believe it or not, only a few minutes later my phone rang—and it was Rich. He was nervous, didn't know how to come out and say it, but he finally did. He missed me. I hesitated in telling him I was thinking the same thing. *We're on very dangerous ground here*, I thought. But I told him. Another thing we had no qualms agreeing about was, "Now what?"

It was an emotional roller coaster, to say the least. I had never expected, anticipated, or predicted that I would put myself in such a situation. I knew I could walk away or face the music. Rich's marriage had been in a shambles for a couple of years. They didn't have any children, and I knew he had been talking about leaving for a while. None of this justified it, though, because at that time we had only been friends. Now things were different.

For the next month or so, we rationalized, theorized, and figured out what lay ahead. It was difficult. Then one day, out of the blue, he called me.

"I've left," was all he said.

I was stunned, since I had never asked him to leave his marriage. But to be honest, I was thrilled. Rich was everything I could have asked for, and most important, he had become my best friend. Obviously, the fallout was distressing, if expected. I was a home-wrecking whore (one of the nicer terms), and it was a big scandal in Mayberry since we had both worked there.

I didn't care; I was truly happy for the first time in years. Rich took to my daughter, who was only three years old at the time, as if she were his own. A year later, we married, and less than a year after that, our daughter was born. Over a decade later, we remain best friends and partners, and we still spend every free moment together. I simply fell in love and remain happy.

But *those* bunnies are still out there—overpopulating at an alarming rate. So my eyes will always remain open.

PART III

Dark Days Behind the Badge

CHAPTER 10

Just One of the Guys

WHEN I FIRST started as one of two females in a city unaccustomed to modern twentieth-century policing, I came in with an overwhelming naïveté. The prospect that my dream had actually come true—that I would be putting on my own police blues, be issued my own weapon, and be given a badge —blinded me to all the obstacles that lay ahead. Of course, at the time I didn't even know what these obstacles were. Just getting hired had been an obstacle. I thought that was probably going to be the worst of it—clearly, I had no idea what was coming.

In Ohio, all cities fall under the civil service code. So if you want to be a police officer, you simply take a written test and are ranked according to your score. I had taken several tests already and scored fairly well, but this was a time when affirmative action was given serious weight. Lawsuits were filed by several civil rights groups, and several times I was shunted to the side in favor of minority applicants.

It was frustrating to me. I remember arguing the point with a local black defense attorney when I worked one summer in a law office. To an extent, I could see his point, but he refused to see mine. What I couldn't understand was why any city would lower its standards of quality to accommodate skin color. There were plenty of black police officers on that particular city's police force, men who had been hired the same way everyone else had. They had scored well on the test, passed the physical and psychological exams, and become cops—it was pretty simple. So if these officers could do it, why lower the standards for others? I was hit in the face with this particular dilemma less than six months later.

My Police Academy commander happened to be a high-ranking officer at a smaller city about thirty minutes from my own. In a brave attempt to become progressive (in the 1990s), this particular city wanted to hire a female officer. According to the commander, the chief of police of this particular city had researched the possibility extensively and determined that hiring two females would be better than one (the theory being that they could keep each other company).

I remember the commander calling me at home with an offer I couldn't refuse—yet I did. The offer was that I simply had to pass a written test and my name would be added to a separate list of females, two of whom would be hired. I knew that being hired by a department through a set of different standards would work against me in the end. I had to earn my spot like everyone else in order to earn respect from my male counterparts. So I refused his offer.

Subsequently, I took the test along with everyone else (male and female) and did very well. Out of a pool of two hundred applicants, I ranked eighth—the highest female score.

Now all I had to do was pass the physical agility test, the psychological test, the polygraph, and the background check to be chosen for one of the four available positions. Another female—Lolita—had ranked just below me, and I had heard through the rumor mill that she was one of their favorites. At this point, I began to worry how I was going to manage moving up four spots. The physical agility test just about killed me. I had just had a baby and was in the worst possible shape. However, I gritted my teeth and made it through the obstacle course with a few seconds to spare. Lolita flunked her test. Normally, that would be it, but they told her she could take the test again. I remember talking to her, and she didn't want to do it again. Being a compassionate person, I cheered her on and told her to go for it. If I'd known then what I know now, I would've handled that day quite differently.

Everything from that point on seemed to be smooth sailing. In fact, according to my own calculations, I had moved up the list to second place. Several others above me had been disqualified for various reasons ranging from failed background checks to failed psychological exams. Now it was simply a matter of waiting—and the wait seemed to take forever.

At a street fair I ran into a friend of mine, and another applicant, and received some rather dismal news. According to him, the department had officially filled the four available slots, and Lolita had been granted one of them; I had not. I was devastated. Apparently, the department had decided to forgo the two-female theory and hire only one.

Fortunately, this rumor proved to be short-lived. The department called me several weeks later, confirmed that I *had* been ranked second, and offered me a job. Lolita got the fourth slot; go figure. All in all, the department fared well in the minority category: They filled their four slots with a Hispanic male, two females, and a white male.

I remember the day they officially offered me the job. It was the end of summer, and as I drove away from the police department in my beat-up Saturn, I blasted Supertramp on the radio, hit my steering wheel, and screamed out loud. Yes! I had finally become a full-time police officer.

Lolita and I became instant celebrities in the small city. The department paraded us around to radio shows and newspaper interviews to document their "progressiveness." I recall driving in my car one day and hearing a Cleveland radio station air a commercial that started out with, "Hey, did ya hear two female police officers were hired in Mayberry? Times are a-changin' and so are our new car prices...."

I laughed out loud.

It took only one day on the job to realize that some of the male officers absolutely did not want us there. Almost everyone there knew my family, and I like to think I was cut a little slack because of that. Later on, though, it wouldn't have mattered if I were the president's daughter, there was simply no mercy.

Unfortunately for Lolita and me, one of the officers who didn't want us there. After our probationary period, Lieutenant Ray Roberts, became our commander. He was old school, having started his police career in the late 1970s when female "officers" wore skirts and high heels and worked the radio as dispatchers. Lieutenant Roberts had declared openly that "the only thing a female officer brings to a police department is problems and pregnancy"—and he allowed his opinion to affect his supervision of Lolita and me.

Needless to say, Lolita and I quickly bonded. Two fish out of water, flopping around a male locker room, we shared our fears, thoughts, concerns, laughter, and friendship as if we were sisters. It didn't last, but it was certainly helpful while it did.

Our probation lasted approximately one year, during which time we could be fired on the spot without cause. If we made it the full year, we would be admitted to the Ohio Patrolmen's Benevolent Association and protected. In fact, another officer who had been hired shortly before we were came into work on the last day of his probationary period and was promptly fired. It was a farce: He was a good officer but had a personality conflict with a powerful lieutenant. That officer's termination caused me to think about what might lie ahead for me during my probation.

At the time, I couldn't think of anything that might cause my own termination. I had learned what to expect, what not to expect, and how to deal (and not deal) with things. Although I never saw it that way then, I had been subjected to what outsiders would consider exceptional sexual harassment. To me, there's no such thing as sexual harassment unless the person on the receiving end is offended. I was not.

Each officer, whether on probation or not, was subjected to an extensive work performance evaluation every four months. Whenever evaluation time came around, there was a lot of bitching and moaning over low scores and who got the highest score. In my opinion, the evaluations were worthless. No disciplinary action was taken for those who received low scores (which were rarely given anyway, since no supervisor wanted to be considered the asshole who gave his guys low scores).

During my probationary period and field training, I was under Lieutenant Steve Taylor and Sergeant Chris Powell. Lieutenant Taylor was pretty much the most powerful man in the department, and he was also the Police Academy commander who had first approached me about the job. He would undoubtedly become the next chief of police and had strong relationships with the higher-ups of Ohio's law enforcement. Sergeant Powell was a humorless, no-nonsense Boy Scout who saw his job in terms of black and white—a combination that makes for a pretty unsatisfactory cop. Sergeant Powell was a citizen's nightmare: There were no breaks, no warnings, no sympathy, and little compassion.

As my first four-month evaluation drew near, I started to get nervous. I got myself so worked up that when the day finally arrived, I reported to the supervisor's office feeling queasy and short of breath.

Lieutenant Taylor and Sergeant Powell sat facing me behind the supervisor's desk, both of them stone-faced. *Uh-oh, this isn't good*, I thought. Lieutenant Taylor, when you were on his good side, had a pretty outgoing personality, so this was unusual for him. My stomach was tied in knots as I sat in the "hot" seat in front of the two commanding officers.

"I'm sorry, Stacy, but we were hoping to see a little better performance," Lieutenant Taylor started out as he handed me my evaluation.

I gulped and looked down at the paper, hands trembling.

The evaluations were broken down into several sections, including work performance, radio professionalism, uniform and cruiser maintenance, and knowledge of the job. Scores were ranked 1–5, 5 being the highest. To my knowledge, no one had ever received a score below 3. A few things jumped out at me:

Uniform/Cruiser Maintenance: Score: 1½

Comments: Officer Wendling's [I kept my maiden name] *cruiser is frequently dirty, her windows foggy, and she fails to maintain pride in her work environment. Her uniform is frequently wrinkled, and she fails to polish her shoes on a consistent basis. Her hair, fingernails, and makeup are usually to department standards, which offsets the low score in the other areas.*

This has got to be a joke! I thought, fighting the lump in my throat. I was downright anal about my appearance. I shined my shoes not once but three times a week, and I pressed my uniforms daily. If my cruiser had so much as a speck of dirt on it, I rinsed it off. I called the supervisors on my opinion.

"This is a joke, right?" I tried to break into my signature grin.

They remained stoic. "No, this isn't a joke."

I believed them, particularly since I knew Sergeant Powell would never take part in a joke like this. He simply didn't have it in him. Fighting tears, I kept reading, and it didn't get any better.

Radio Traffic/Professionalism: Score: 2

Comments: Although Officer Wendling does her best to give as much information as needed, she tends to ramble on, leaving little time for other officers' traffic and dispatch emergency. She needs extensive work in her verbiage and vocabulary in this area.

Summary of Work Performance: Score: 2½

Comments: Officer Wendling comes to work every day with a positive attitude and ready to work. She has an impeccable knowledge of the law but fails to apply it to her daily duties. Her reports lack the necessary information and are subpar: Her arrests, albeit few, seem to border on questionable. We don't doubt that Officer Wendling will be able to perform her duties as a police officer, but with extensive training and leadership, we feel her potential will lead to an average—or just below—officer at best.

The rest of the evaluation was similar. By the time I finished reading it, my heart was thumping in my chest, I had sweat streaming down my face, and it was all I could do not to bawl. *I have tried so hard!* my head screamed. *This isn't right! I did everything I was supposed to do!* Apparently, knowing I was on the verge of a breakdown, the two supervisors alerted me to the fact that the jig was up. Just as their smiles broke across their faces, I noticed the little red light of the videocamera hidden behind Sergeant Powell's head. It *was* a joke!

"Here's your *real* eval," Lieutenant Taylor said, laughing as he handed me another packet of papers.

The *real* evaluation was, obviously, much better. I had nothing but 4's and 5's as my scores: impeccable appearance, clear knowledge of the law, airtight arrests, blah, blah, blah. It didn't matter then. I was so upset from the fake evaluation that I handed back the papers, excused myself, and walked out of the office. I remember another sergeant was standing in the hallway and had overheard the entire meeting.

"Let me know when you file the lawsuit, I'll be sure and testify for you. That was pure bullshit," he said.

I ignored him and kept walking. I refused to cry in front of anyone. Trudging down the hall, sweating, shaking, and utterly decomposed, I headed to the bathroom, where I lost it. All I could think about was my baby. During that "joke," the only thing on my mind was how I was going to take care of her. I was going to be fired.

Finally, I got myself together. I knew I had to play the game, so I threw some water on my face, took a deep breath, and headed back to the supervisor's office.

"Okay, so you got me." I smiled and poked at the lieutenant.

"Here, keep this as a memento." Lieutenant Taylor handed me the videotape of the entire incident. "Yeah, we got you. Your face was classic!"

Throughout the conversation, Sergeant Powell remained silent. However, later in the shift, he called me on the radio and asked me to meet him at the community park. When I pulled up next to his cruiser, I knew something was wrong.

"Look, Stacy, I want to apologize." He looked me directly in the eye. "Ya know me. I don't do stuff like that, but Steve pretty much made me do it. I'm sorry, and I hope you don't think badly of me for that."

I gave him my programmed response: "Oh, for crying out loud, I thought it was funny, Sarg! You know you guys don't need to worry about me, I'm just one of the guys!"

Inside, I was still reeling from the experience and trying to calm myself down. I didn't for a minute doubt that Sergeant Powell was uncomfortable with the whole joke, but what could he do? His lieutenant had told him he was going to do it and that was that.

I had walked out of my first marriage with just the clothing on my back—shorts and a T-shirt—and the baby with the baby bag. It was the best decision I've ever made. That was the day I decided I would no longer put up with anyone's bullshit, no matter what it cost. My sole purpose at that point was making the best life possible for my child.

I garnered overwhelming support from my co-workers when my divorce was finalized. They were my brothers and defended and protected me throughout. It was an amazing feeling, something I hadn't experienced before.

However, there were times when they weren't all that sympathetic or helpful. For instance, I walked into roll call one day only to learn that a bet had been placed on the dry erase board regarding which cop would be the first to sleep with me after the divorce was finalized. Apparently, the betting reached some fairly high numbers. Since I was adamant about never "playing" where I worked, I told them all they were dumb-asses who had just thrown their money out the window. I would sleep with none of them, period. I'm proud to say that was a vow I stuck with.

At any rate, my probation year came and went without termination, and I rejoiced. I had made it. I was in a nice town house in an upscale neighborhood in Mansfield, just me and my baby girl, Brooke. I had a reliable and affordable babysitter and a secure job with fantastic benefits. And I was starting to date again. Life was good.

At this point, Lolita and I were working for Lieutenant Roberts, whose disdain—subtle at first—grew more obvious over time.

Certain little things I initially brushed off: For instance, once when I was running lights and sirens to an emergency call and asked the dispatcher for the cross-streets that intersected the residence I was going to—a standard request in policing—Lieutenant Roberts grabbed her radio mike and screamed at me to "get a map, 140!" (I was identified by my unit number, 140.)

Although humiliated, I ignored him. Clearly, I wasn't going to pull over and scrutinize my map while responding to an emergency. Another time, during rush hour, he ordered Lolita and me to direct traffic downtown. The traffic lights were working just fine, and his order was unheard of—we were absolutely humiliated.

Eventually, however, his actions became too serious to be ignored—like the time Lolita stopped a car with five male occupants, several who had arrest warrants, and Lieutenant Roberts ordered the officers responding to her stop to "disregard." Essentially, he called off her backup.

This became common. I was on scene at a bar fight, and Lieutenant Roberts ordered all responding units to discontinue, told them he would back me up. But he never showed up, leaving me to release several people who should have been arrested, simply for my own safety.

Things came to a head when I was sent to a domestic violence call where the husband was barricaded with a shotgun.

The only available officer was headed to the city hospital to ride with the ambulance while they transported a mental patient to the state psychiatric facility—a god-awful job we had to do at the time. That officer told the dispatcher he was discontinuing his trip to the hospital and would be en route to assist me.

Lieutenant Roberts screamed across the radio at the other officer to "disregard" me and continue to his nonemergency call. Luckily for me, the officer ignored the order and came to my aid, along with a county sheriff's deputy. The husband in the domestic was alarmingly violent. We ultimately disarmed him, and he was taken to jail—something I couldn't possibly have managed on my own.

Perhaps the worst hell I endured during this period occurred after I responded to a call involving an unruly juvenile. Arriving in front of the appropriate trailer, I could hear the teenage girl inside screaming at the top of her lungs. Her mother opened the door for me, and when I went inside, the girl was throwing a fit. I promptly took her by the arm and escorted her outside until she calmed down. The call was insignificant to me until a few days later. Lieutenant Roberts called me into his office and informed me I was officially under investigation for excessive use of force and unlawful detainment of a teenage girl. I had no idea what he was talking about until he handed me the complaint form (signed by the chief of police, no less).

The complaint stated that the teenage girl I referred to above came to the police department with her mother, alleging that I had dragged her by the hair out the front door of their trailer, down the steps, and slapped her across the face, all without making a physical arrest. I was floored and actually looked around for a videocamera, hoping this was another joke.

Unfortunately, there was no videocamera.

Turned out I was the first officer in almost ten years to undergo a criminal investigation. Outstanding. I always liked to make a grand impression and be first in everything, but this wasn't what I'd signed up for. I knew complaints were filed against officers daily, but rarely did they reach this level. And the chief had signed off on it! I was terrified, sick, angry, and shocked. To make matters worse, Lieutenant Roberts conducted his investigation on my shift *on the radio,* frequently calling out addresses and referring them to the "internal investigation," for me and everyone else to hear. He was taunting me. There had been another officer with me at the call during the entire incident, and he had yet to be questioned.

One of the turning points came the day Lolita stopped a car full of scumbags. We were familiar with the occupants, and they normally had warrants or were out committing some type of crime. When she stopped the car, they pulled over into a local pizza shop parking lot. Backing Lolita up on the car stop, I was a little miffed when the pizza shop owner came out screaming at us.

"Get these fucking cruisers out of my parking lot! This is bad for my business!" he screamed.

Since the car Lolita had stopped had about five male occupants in it, and she and I were the only two officers on site, we certainly didn't need this distraction to jeopardize our safety.

Keeping my eyes on the car, I told the pizza owner to stand to the side and I would speak to him when we were finished. That merely incited him more. Finally, I looked at him and told him that if he didn't back away and shut his mouth, he was going to be arrested for obstructing. He stormed back into his shop, and all was well—until later, almost at the end of my shift.

That was when the dispatcher informed Lieutenant Roberts that the pizza shop owner was on the phone. And, she added pointedly, "he wants to file a complaint."

I knew this dispatcher didn't like Lolita or me and was often on the phone with Lieutenant Roberts giving him an update on what we were doing. She undoubtedly relished the thought of broadcasting over the airwaves that Lolita and I were looking at another complaint.

By the time I arrived at the police department to take off

my gear and go home for the night, I was feeling sick at the thought of having to face yet another investigation. I will never forget that night driving home—I broke. I was five minutes out of the department's parking lot and I started sobbing to the point that I was ill. So ill, in fact, that I barely had time to stop my car before vomiting in my daughter's book bag on the passenger-seat floor.

Regardless, I muddled through. The investigation regarding the teenage girl was officially closed after she and her mother admitted to a detective sergeant that they had lied about the complaints against me. They were merely pissed off about the way the police department handled another case they were involved in, and this was their way of getting back. The department never filed charges against them, and I never received an apology. It didn't matter, though; I did my best to keep my chin up and do my job. And all the while, Lieutenant Roberts continued his mission to ruin Lolita and me.

I kept my mouth shut. However, it was my male counterparts—and friends—who had enough. It was *they* who went to the police chief and complained about Lieutenant Roberts's treatment of Lolita and me. Lieutenant Roberts was immediately notified that *he* was under an official internal investigation.

It would be logical to think that things would get better after that, but they didn't.

During Lieutenant Roberts's investigation, the department ran into another snag. The famed, liked, and well-known Lieutenant Taylor had a complaint filed against him for stalking.

A married Police Academy student, whom he acknowledged having an affair with, accused him of stalking her, breaking into her house, and threatening her. The media coverage of the well-known and respected lieutenant ranged from Cleveland to Columbus—it was phenomenal. Little did I know I was about to be thrown right into the middle of it.

Our department had a contract with one of the area's low-income apartment complexes. An officer could live there, rent-free, for the sole purpose of deterring crime. Naturally, the apartment turned into a "sex getaway" where officers could take their girlfriends during their lunch breaks, after hours, or whenever—a place where their wives wouldn't catch them. I couldn't have cared less at the time, it was none of my business, but it was Lieutenant Taylor who negotiated the apartment contract for the police department (he was, of course, sleeping with the apartment complex's manager). So when the state decided to come in and do an audit, Lieutenant Taylor panicked. One officer was using the apartment off and on, rotating between his wife and girlfriend (clearly confused as to whom he preferred). When Lieutenant Taylor was notified of the state's audit, he told the officer to "get your shit out of the apartment ASAP!"

The officer didn't.

After several requests, Lieutenant Taylor resorted to having a female make several "anonymous" phone calls to the officer's wife, informing her of her husband's "extracurricular" activities. When asked by the academy student he was having an affair with, he told her that he'd had "one of the female officers make the phone calls."

The officer in the apartment and the academy student both filed formal complaints against Lieutenant Taylor around the same time. Thus, I found myself whisked into the Office of Internal Affairs and grilled about my relationship with Lieutenant Taylor.

I was horrified.

I wanted nothing to do with such a high-profile police investigation. Lieutenant Taylor was a friend of my father's, and I had known him since I was little. I didn't want to hurt him, but I wasn't going to lie, either. I remember the questioning as if it were yesterday.

Internal Affairs Detective: Officer Wendling, there are a lot of rumors going around that you were, or are, sexually involved with Lieutenant Taylor. This is an official investigation and you are required to give a truthful answer. If your answer is later evidenced to be untruthful, you can be disciplined—up to termination. Have you, in the past or present, ever engaged in a sexual relationship with Lieutenant Taylor?

My answer: Absolutely not. I have *never* been involved with Lieutenant Taylor sexually. He was a friend of my father's, we maintained a friendship, and that is the full extent of our relationship.

Internal Affairs Detective: Officer Wendling, did you ever, on occasion, make an anonymous phone call to the spouse of Officer X informing her that her husband was engaging in extramarital affairs?

My answer: No, I did not.

Internal Affairs Detective: Officer Wendling, are you aware of any extramarital affairs that Lieutenant Taylor is currently engaged in, at this time?

My answer: Yes, I am.

Internal Affairs Detective: Would you please give me the names and circumstances of these affairs that you allegedly have knowledge of?

My answer: Lieutenant Taylor is currently involved with Holland County sheriff's deputy Anne Sebastian. She was in my Police Academy and a good friend who confided in me frequently regarding her affair with Lieutenant Taylor. In fact, prior to taking the state exam, she claimed they had sex in his office at Ohio State University. As we departed for the Ohio Police Officer's Training Academy in London, Ohio, she showed me a white spot on her uniform shirt and claimed it was semen from Lieutenant Taylor, as they had just had sex minutes before. I spoke with her on the phone two days ago, and she claimed that they had engaged in sexual intercourse in her van while parked in a parking lot, and laughed, as a uniformed officer sat nearby doing his papcrwork. To my knowledge, they are still involved in a sexual relationship at the time of this interview. That's all I know.

Internal Affairs Detective: Officer Wendling, is there anything else that you have knowledge of or would like to add to this interview?

My answer: No, sir.

When I left the interview, I was shaken, angry, scared, and rattled. I wasn't a rat, but I had a daughter to take care of and I'd be damned if I lost my job for Lieutenant Taylor. Maybe I'd have been a little more discreet in my disclosures if he hadn't brought me into the whole mess by telling his "lover" that either Lolita or I had made the phone calls. His lies might have cost me my job.

I remember he'd once told me that a nearby sheriff's department was starting a rumor that he and I were sleeping together. I came unglued and demanded to know where he'd heard the rumor, and he'd refused to tell me. I later realized that it was he who had started the rumor.

Ultimately, they found out that the female who had made the anonymous phone calls was a Child Protective Services caseworker whom Lieutenant Taylor was also sleeping with. She was subsequently fired, and I never received an apology—again.

Lieutenant Taylor, a man I had known since I was a child, a man I had respected, was ultimately indicted for burglary, among other charges, and sent to prison. I was there the day they brought him into the department in handcuffs. Many of the guys laughed and taunted him, but I didn't think it was funny. I found the situation profoundly sad. What could possibly be funny about one of your own being carted off to jail? It made all of us look bad.

So that was our department's "summer of hell," as several newspapers termed it. The bad part about it was that the chief of police—a spineless man who didn't want the bad press of having two lieutenants criminally charged in one summer— deliberately expedited Lieutenant Roberts's investigation to avoid prolonging the media scrutiny.

The department's manner of disciplining Lieutenant Roberts began with removing him as a watch commander on Lolita and my shift. At the time, however, termination was still a distinct possibility. On his last night as our supervisor, on the midnight shift, Lieutenant Roberts assigned Lolita and me to the same zone (although we worked the same shift, he had never before assigned us to the same area, or zone). We had no idea what was in store for us that night, the danger that awaited us—at the hands of one of our own.

THE NIGHT TURNED OUT to be fairly quiet. Lolita and I spent most of it holed up together, talking about the imminent transfer of Lieutenant Roberts and what a weight would be lifted off our shoulders once he was gone. We were thankful our superiors were finally going to bat for us. We talked about how nice it would be to actually be able to do our jobs for once.

Then the call was dispatched across the radio to Lolita and me.

What occurred over the next hour was believed by some and disregarded by others. The bottom line was that was the night Lieutenant Roberts planned to murder Lolita and me and make it look like an on-duty homicide by an unknown burglar.

It sounds insane, I know. But just imagine how insane we felt thinking it, knowing deep inside that it was actually happening.

As Lolita and I sat chatting away in the early hours of the morning, the dispatcher came across the radio and sent us to a report of an "open door" at a nearby factory. The call had come in "anonymously." No big deal; that sort of thing happens all the time. Someone drives by a business at three o'clock in the morning, sees a door wide open, and calls the cops. We respond, go in the business, clear the building of potential burglars, call the owner to secure the door, and go about the rest of our shift. It's simple.

This night was anything but simple. The factory was located less than a mile from where we sat gabbing away. As we pulled our cruisers near the building with the headlights off, just as we'd been taught, we were shocked to see Lieutenant Roberts already in the parking lot. What attracted our attention was that he had his spotlight on the open door and his gun out of its holster.

Why was that odd? Because Lieutenant Roberts was known for being unsafe, brazen, stupid, and tactically inept.

For us to spot Lieutenant Roberts in such a posture of watchfulness and caution raised some red flags. As we exited our cruisers, guns drawn, Lieutenant Roberts walked swiftly through the open door and turned right. We were less than seconds behind him in entering the door.

However, when we entered and turned right, there was dead silence. No Lieutenant Roberts, nothing but a huge warehouse full of wooden "skids," or planks. He had simply disappeared. There was a small light by the entrance to the warehouse, and Lolita and I stood there, exposed for the entire world to see. It was the most uncomfortable feeling I can ever remember.

I could see the farthest wall of the warehouse where there was an exit door, and it was closed. We called out to the lieutenant and received no response. There were stacks of skids piled in rows fifteen feet high, so there was a lot of searching to do, and we could only assume that he was walking the rows. But he absolutely would have heard us call out. Yes, there was the possibility that something had happened to him—but that never crossed our minds. However, after a few seconds, something incredibly strange happened.

At the time, I wasn't paying much attention to Lolita; gun drawn, I was scanning my surroundings in search of Lieutenant Roberts or a potential burglar. We had been standing there for less than a minute when I was completely overcome by a horrific sense that I was in extreme danger. As cops, we are taught over and over to trust our instincts, but until then I had usually brushed off my "red flags" as paranoia. But not that night. Breaking out in a cold sweat, I noticed a dark corner directly behind me. Trying to control my breathing, I backed slowly into the darkened corner and kept my gun right in front of me, ready to fire.

The dispatcher was calling us continuously to check our status, and Lieutenant Roberts wasn't answering his radio.

She also informed us that she was unable to get hold of the factory owner. Lolita and I were on our own.

Since I was completely occupied with getting myself into a safe position, I disregarded Lolita—a major faux pas for a cop. But I was sure she'd think I was nuts for acting this way. Until I saw her.

She was just outside the lighted area, crouched behind a pile of skids. Her face had paled, and like me, she was sweating profusely. Just then, we locked eyes and she mouthed, "He's going to whack us," alerting me to the fact that I wasn't nuts. Her instincts were telling her the same thing, and she was scared.

I nodded and then gestured toward the door we had come in, signaling that I'd cover her while she made a run for it. I was hidden in the dark, she wasn't. He was out there somewhere, in the darkness of the warehouse, waiting for us; there wasn't a doubt in my mind. Then I noticed that the door on the farthest wall was now open (I hadn't heard a thing), and I put it all together. I believed Lieutenant Roberts made the anonymous call for the sole purpose of luring Lolita and me to the warehouse. While there, he intended to use a "throw down" gun (one that wasn't registered) to shoot us both and claim it was a burglar who subsequently escaped through the rear entrance. Yes, I sound like a lunatic, but I will go to my grave believing that was to have been our fate that night.

As Lolita was about to make a run for the door, a miracle occurred. We heard voices and several subjects coming through the same door we had entered to get into the factory. Three people emerged, yelling, "Hello?"

Lolita and I remained silent in our covers. But from nowhere, Lieutenant Roberts emerged, sweating and not acknowledging the people. He headed right for the door and left, ignoring them. The people looked at one another in disbelief as Lolita and I came out of our hiding spots and identified the subjects as the owners of the factory.

The reason the dispatcher couldn't get hold of them was that they actually had a police scanner they listened to 24/7. They had heard the call dispatched about their own factory, so they'd left immediately to respond. They lived about twenty-five minutes away. Clearly, Lieutenant Roberts hadn't counted on that.

After the owners secured the building and left, Lolita and I walked to our cars slowly, trying to comprehend what had just happened. I distinctly remember her vomiting along the side of her cruiser as we wondered if we had completely lost our minds or if, in fact, our own lieutenant had just planned to kill us that night. It was a hard pill to swallow.

In the days that followed, Lolita told this incident to another officer (one she subsequently began sleeping with), and he flipped. He immediately went to the detective bureau and made a complaint. He told other officers, and they actually believed us. The detective bureau started an investigation and called Lolita and me in, asking us to give statements on a tape recorder.

We refused. We both knew the consequences of making such claims. We would be deemed crazy, vindictive bitches, and it wasn't worth it. The higher-ups wouldn't possibly believe us. But the internal affairs officer coaxed and promised us that something would actually be done this time if we gave our honest statements, and we believed him.

Therefore, Lolita and I sat in front of a tape recorder and gave our play-by-play of the night we believed Lieutenant Roberts planned to "whack us" over his possible termination and ongoing investigation. At the end of my statement, the internal affairs officer said to me, "I undoubtedly believe both of you. Not only am I going to see to it that he is fired, but I want to see him in prison."

What was the outcome? you ask. You guessed it: Absolutely nothing. Lieutenant Roberts hired a bigwig attorney who threatened to run the department through the mud for a variety of things past and present. The chief cowered and relented, and less than six months later I was back under the command of Lieutenant Roberts.

Welcome to the wonderful world of law enforcement.

Funny—soon after, the entire shift had complaints against Lieutenant Roberts, and they all decided we should each put our complaints in writing. What was my response?

I don't think so.

CHAPTER 11

Rumors

I'M NOT A huge fan of celebrities, but I'll give them credit for one thing: The best of them have developed a thick skin, which enables them to withstand the overwhelming public scrutiny and constant media speculation. I simply couldn't handle it. I've always been someone who takes rumors and criticism to heart.

I'm certainly no stranger to the rumor mill. In fact, I couldn't begin to count the number of times I've been subjected to gossip. However, that never made it any easier as a police officer.

I've always been a straight shooter. If I've done something questionable, I have always stepped up and acknowledged it. It became a topic of discussion that when I met Rich, he was still married. This is true, although it's not something I'm proud of. Yet I don't consider my relationship with Rich a misstep, I consider it a blessing. And we've got a beautiful seven-year-old daughter to show for it.

The bottom line is, when I'm wrong, I'm wrong. If I've done something, I've never seen the point in trying to hide it. My father always told me, "No one likes a liar." And I've taken his advice to heart.

Once, when I was in high school, I and other members of the cheerleading squad were smoking in one of the "unpatrolled" bathrooms. Needless to say, I remember looking up and seeing a teacher peering over the stall and we were all hauled to the principal's office. None of us had a cigarette in our hand at the time but, obviously, the bathroom was filled with a haze the likes of Cheech and Chong had rarely seen. Subsequently, we were questioned one by one.

I was the only one who admitted to smoking. The others denied it. As a result, I was thrown off the cheerleading squad; a true punishment for my honesty. Granted, I could've lied like the others and kept my prominent status but, as far as I was concerned, it was about character.

From that point on, I was treated like a pariah. One day I was in the hallway talking to one of my cheerleading friends and the advisor of the cheerleading squad (a biology teacher) walked by, stopped, acted as if I weren't there, and said, "Watch the company you keep." I was horrified. I couldn't believe that a grown woman would be so hateful to a 15-year-old girl. How naïve I was.

Maybe I should have lied. But, then again, who would I have become: a materialistic, appearance-obsessed, high school cheerleader? Big deal.

I thought for sure my dad, who was raising me alone, would

flip out at my suspension and ejection from the cheerleading squad. Rather, he was totally on my side. I remember that he called the principal and got into a heated argument about persecution for telling the truth—what kind of message does that send? To this day, Dad still tells the "smoking cheerleader" story—a story of honesty.

In my opinion, there's nothing worse than a liar. I've known these types of people all my life, and I've always kept them at arm's length.

When I began my quest to become a police officer, the rumors intensified; it was astonishing.

By the time all was said and done, I had posed in *Playboy* magazine, posed nude on the Internet, slept with a high-ranking lieutenant to get my job, and committed criminal acts while on duty. Let's take one at a time.

I began modeling when I was five years old. It started out at local department stores, local print catalogs, that sort of thing. My mother thought I was destined to be some famous actress or model. Inside, I was dying to be a cop.

A year after I graduated from high school, I entered a "new face" competition for a Cleveland modeling agency and won. The prize was a trip to New York City to meet with the world's top modeling and talent agencies. It was a surreal time in my life. Everyone had such high hopes. My stepfather even drew up a contract that appointed him my business manager. Everyone was positive I would make it big—and make a ton of money.

The day I landed in New York City, I received the shock of my life. I was surrounded by beautiful women, women who made me look like a corn-fed plain Jane from Ohio. I was confident when I boarded the plane to New York, but by the time I came home, I had become an insecure, babbling idiot with an ego the size of a pinhead. It was 1993, the dawn of the "waif" models. Kate Moss was a modeling superstar. At five feet six inches and 120 pounds, I was "curvier" than most. At that point, one needed to see ribs sticking out to make it.

Not only that, I was sabotaged. The other model wannabes were relentless, and I was a dumb, naïve girl from Ohio. There was a model who I thought took me under her wing, only now I realize how wrong I was. I'll call her Sara.

Sara would spend quite a bit of time with me, giving me tips on how to walk on the runway, how to wear my hair. Right before a swimsuit presentation on the runway, I was waiting in the hallway for my roommate. Sara looked at me and said, "You have to wear your hair in a tight bun—they want to see your face."

Frantic, I ran into my room and threw my hair into a bun that could deflect any object if thrown. As I entered the ballroom where the show was being held, I saw all the other models with their hair down, and it was too late to fix my own; I was next on the runway.

Needless to say, it went downhill from there. I clearly didn't fit in with these other girls. For one thing, I wouldn't sleep with someone for a modeling job; and for another, I liked to eat: two factors that would quash anyone's modeling dreams. My roommate would frequently be gone overnight; she would blatantly tell all of us about her sexual escapes with modeling agents. And I knew I was with the wrong crowd the day a few of us stopped in for a bite to eat at a small café on Broadway. While they ordered Diet Cokes, I helped myself to a slice of garlic bread with melted cheese. They were horrified.

"Do you have any idea how many calories that has in it?" said one, rolling her eyes.

"I don't care, I'm hungry," I fired back.

As the table grew silent and looks were exchanged, I noticed two New York City policemen standing outside the window of the café. Quietly pushing away my garlic bread (I had lost my appetite), I excused myself and went outside. I noticed immediately that one of the officers carried a "wheel gun," something that was on the way out in the early 1990s. I spoke with them for about fifteen to twenty minutes, talking about guns, crime, and the like. It was the best time I can remember having during the dark period I visited New York City.

One night, the manager of the Waldorf=Astoria Hotel (where we stayed) treated us to an evening on the town, complete with a limousine and VIP access to the hottest clubs in the city. At the time, the hot tickets in town were to the China Club and Limelight. Eddie Murphy, Sylvester Stallone, and other celebrities were there, but I wasn't fazed. We wound up at Chippendales. While the other models were on the dance floor trying to line up a date, I was at the back of the club, talking to the young waiter about what college courses he had enrolled in.

It grew much, much worse. When callbacks came in, I was one of the few who didn't receive one. I was too curvy, my hands were too big, my feet were too big, I was too old (at nineteen), I didn't have the right "look." I was devastated.

The day before I left, I was sitting at the fountain in the Waldorf=Astoria, looking at the ground in a state of shock. I couldn't believe I had come there with such high hopes.

"Excuse me," said a woman.

"Yes?" I looked up.

"My name is Sharon Churchill. I'm a reporter for *Allure* magazine. Can I talk to you for a moment?"

I nodded.

She proceeded to tell me she was doing an article on the modeling industry, modeling scams and such, and wanted to know about my own experience. I gladly obliged.

Two months after I returned home from New York, I was shocked when *Allure* called me about the article. They wanted to fly me back to New York City for a photo shoot to accompany the article.

For a day, I actually felt like a celebrity. I was picked up in a limousine, put up in a swanky hotel, and had an assistant assigned to me for the day. When the magazine came out, I thought I looked pretty awful, but the entire experience was fun. Still, those experiences in New York certainly fueled some rumors when I entered law enforcement. My fully clothed photo shoot for *Allure* turned into a *Playboy* centerfold spread within law enforcement gossip circles.

Even after I'd been a cop for years, the hits kept coming. I went to work one day to learn there were naked photographs of me on the Internet. No one had actually seen them; they'd just heard the rumor from a couple of gossip-hungry dispatchers in the next county. Regardless, I was horrified. I had everyone I knew scouring the Internet for hours in search of the mysterious photos. I had never had a photograph taken when I was naked, so I immediately assumed someone had Photoshopped my face onto someone else's body. Finally, the root of the rumor surfaced.

My cousin had been attending college at Ohio State University and was part of a sorority. They had done a calendar where they were all in their pajamas. Not negligees, but full-fledged nightgowns and flannels. Apparently, the women who started the rumor thought it would be funny to "mix things up."

For the most part I ignored rumors, but I also learned that dealing with them head-on and going right to the source usually did the trick. If you're a new officer getting ready to embark on a lifelong career of catching bad guys—beware, it's definitely time to grow a thick skin.

CHAPTER 12

The Wolf Pack Wears Blue

I DIDN'T REALIZE HOW bad things were at first. In the beginning, I was trying only to fit in and be accepted. However,
for years I kept written records of what I saw happening
around (and to) me—primarily for self-protection, in case I
ever became the focus of what I called "the wolf pack."

Wolf packs are commonplace in police departments: I've
worked at five different PDs in my career (three as a police dispatcher), and there was at least one in every department. Led
by a few arrogant, narcissistic, testosterone-driven bullies who
can snap their fingers and rally everyone else to their cause,
the wolf pack exists to make life miserable for its target: an
officer who failed to gather the appropriate information at a
call or maybe made a sexual comment toward another officer's
girlfriend. If you piss off one of these guys, expect the entire
department to be against you; behind closed doors, a few of

your friends might express sympathy, but they'll never be seen talking to you in front of other officers

By the time they're through, their target ends up quitting his job or battling some trumped-up criminal charge—and these thugs sit back with smiles on their faces, pat one another on the back, and say, "We did it again! Got another one out!"

At the Mayberry Police Department, I never expected to become a victim of the wolf pack, but I saw the sheer hell other officers went through and felt it was probably best to be prepared. When I look back at it now, I realize it was a horrible way to have to go to work every day.

It started very subtly, during Lieutenant Steve Taylor's investigation of stalking and burglary. As you read earlier, I was called into the Office of Internal Affairs and grilled about our relationship. The reason I was called in was that the officer who filed the complaint against Lieutenant Taylor was one of the main wolf pack thugs—Officer Mike Harris.

During the investigation, Lieutenant Taylor called me on the radio every single day to meet him during our shift (a call every other officer would hear as well). Since he was my watch commander, I couldn't refuse, but I began to break a sweat every time I heard his voice over the radio. I knew the other officers were grumbling about it. Lieutenant Taylor was "off-limits." No one spoke to him unless they had to, and he had no more "friends." Anyone caught talking to him in a non-work-related way would suffer the wrath of Mike Harris and his pack of wolves.

One time, Lieutenant Taylor called me because he wanted a cigarette. Yes, I could've told him to go buy his own pack, but he was the lieutenant. What the hell was I supposed to do? Luckily, I saw what was coming down the pipe, so each time I met Lieutenant Taylor, I hid a tape recorder in the door of my cruiser and taped every conversation we had. The pack was starting to accuse me of giving Lieutenant Taylor information about the investigation, so when I went into my interview with internal affairs, I was able to disprove this theory with my tapes. They backed off after that—for a while.

Mike Harris and his nephew Brad Harris, also a police officer, blazed a path of broken careers, broken marriages, and near criminal behavior throughout the course of their careers at Mayberry PD. It was Mike Harris's criminal behavior that brought the investigation down on Lieutenant Taylor. It was Lt. Taylor's wife that called exposing Mike's sexual trysts and misuse of the apartment.

Mike took the focus off himself by bullying the administration and accusing Taylor of telephone harassment, which ultimately turned into a burglary and stalking charge. In the end, Mike's own behavior regarding the apartment was never even mentioned.

Brad Harris was just a younger white-trash-bully version of his uncle. It wasn't unusual for him to date women he'd arrested, and he'd start bar fights off duty. Ironically, I was friends with Mike and Brad for several years. I can't say I ever really respected or liked either one, but I got along with them just the same.

As the years went on, I did my best to keep quiet. If I'd hear Mike Harris yell out, "Oh, c'mon, the bitch wanted it!" when talking about a rape victim, I'd merely shake my head and walk away, chalking up his comments to an extremely low IQ. After I got pregnant with my second daughter, Mike went to my sister-in-law, who was the chief's secretary, and said, "That dumb bitch gets knocked up and thinks she can get whatever she wants around here!" At that point, I took notice. Certainly there were some other serious incidents, but I'd like to focus on the ending.

Our captain at the time, Peter Salsgiver, was a jellyfish. If he could go about his day drinking coffee and socializing with nothing else to do, that was precisely the way he wanted it. The chief of police, Ron Hale, was a downright nonentity. If he was even present at the department, he was usually locked in his office watching *Live with Regis and Kelly* episodes. He was simply going to ride out his years doing as little as possible.

The bulk of the problems began when I became head of the police union and Lolita's ongoing affair with another wolf pack member, Kevin Morgan, started to heat up. Their affair used to incense many members of the department, specifically Brad Harris, who hated Lolita. Their blatant display of affection failed to garner the attention of the chief and captain, even though most of their trysts occurred while on duty, and this angered officers who were getting disciplined for trivial things. When a supervisor insisted the department investigate the matter, Captain Salsgiver complied by asking each of them in private if they were having an affair. They denied it, of course, and that was the end of it as far as the administration was concerned. Months later, Kevin Morgan approached the captain and informed him that there had been an affair and that he had lied. Nevertheless, no discipline was issued and the matter was never brought up again.

Like the other officers, I couldn't have cared less if people were sleeping around, but I got tired of picking up Lolita's slack during work hours when she was off meeting Kevin. It also annoyed me that the administration remained oblivious to her true nature. For years she portrayed herself to be a noncussing, nondrinking Stepford wife, when in reality (behind closed doors) she was a foul-mouthed, beer-guzzling badge bunny. We all learned this later when Kevin confessed to the affair. Shortly after I took on the union position, a small storm began brewing under my radar—I was unaware of it. After the dust had settled, I learned that Lolita had been one of the main characters involved in a full-blown sabotage of my career. Like a princess guarding her castle, she wanted no competition among her many paramours. Who knows exactly what "favors" she provided them (the rumors were long and detailed), but she had them swearing their allegiance to her. She was seen several times a week going into the chief's office for a chat and (stupidly) would leave the door open. She was heard bad-mouthing me about everything from my attitude to my intention to seek employment elsewhere. And all the while to my face, I would hear things from her like "We should get the kids together for a playdate! It's been a while!" I was clueless to what she was trying to do.

Then, a major bombshell: Brad Harris filed a formal complaint against another officer who happened to be one of our friends, Nathan Fultz. Brad was actually accusing Nathan of attempting to rape his girlfriend. I had heard Brad grumbling about Nathan over the last few months. Nothing major, just that he was starting to get on his "nerves." Like Lolita, Brad wanted no competition and saw Nathan hot on his trail. I knew Brad was capable of leading the pack against someone, but I never thought he'd go so far as to accuse a fellow officer of a felony. Brad claimed it had happened at a party and that his girlfriend was too fearful to come forward. I thought the claim was laughable until Brad bullied the administration into believing it—something about Nathan taking Brad's girlfriend's hand and putting it on his penis. Attempted rape? I think not. However, they went after Nathan with a vengeance, and I took Nathan's side. Brad's girlfriend had a shady reputation, so it was amazing anyone believed a word she said. It was risky to go against Brad, but in accusing another officer of a felony on a bogus claim, he had gone too far.

Nathan knew the game well enough. He knew they would stop at nothing to pursue him. He had a family, so the notion of quitting was more palatable to him than prison. Obviously, there wasn't much to the claim, because when Nathan resigned, the investigation stopped and no charges were filed. Brad got what he wanted—Nathan gone.

But where I was concerned, the damage was done. I had gone against Brad, so the gloves were off.

Soon after, things began to heat up in the union. Several officers had come to me expressing a desire to switch police unions. They weren't happy with our current one and felt we could do much better. In fact, Brad was one of the officers who approached me about it. After the incident with Nathan, Brad began to accuse me of using the union for my personal gain and successfully convinced everyone to reject every proposal I made. Obviously, his uncle Mike jumped on board.

For the most part, no matter what happened to me, I spent year after year not saying a word to anyone, never lodging an official complaint, always taking things with a grain of salt. I swore I would never be one of those "women" officers who used her gender to negotiate. But the explosion that occurred in the winter of 2002 and early 2003 caused me to reconsider past practices.

It started with a few pot shots here and there, as when Mike Harris kept putting all of his paperwork in my department mailbox. My sister-in-law's mailbox was directly next to mine, so that was where everyone put administrative paperwork: overtime slips, vacation requests, and so on. Every night I came to work, there would be stacks of Mike's papers in my mailbox. I didn't get too excited at first; I simply took them out and threw them in my sister-in-law's box. After months of this, I got fed up. Knowing I couldn't say a word to Mike without his biting my head off, I saw his sergeant, John Price, in the hall one day and said casually, "Hey, Sarg! Would you mind telling Mike to make sure he's putting his paperwork in the right mailbox?" I laughed, and that was the end of it. I didn't know it at the time, but this sergeant (a wolf pack member in charge of Brad and Mike) went to Mike and relayed my message a little differently. He told Mike I was bitching and moaning and wanted Mike to "keep his shit" out of my mailbox.

I was in the squad room one night, getting ready for roll call. The second shift squad was winding down, and their supervisors, Sergeant Price and Lieutenant Damien Phillips, were seated at the watch commander's table, checking reports. Mike came flying into the room, red-faced and yelling at me, "I won't put my *shit* in your mailbox anymore! Got it?"

"Thank you," I said calmly, making a concerted effort to maintain my composure. "You're the only officer in the entire department that does it."

He started walking out of the room, muttering, "Fucking bitch, dumb cunt!"

I looked over at the supervisor's table to see if one of them was going to get a handle on things, but they simply sat there smiling. I couldn't believe it. It was then I realized that Sergeant Price had fueled the fire, and now he was amused. Lieutenant Roberts had been in the hall and overheard Mike's tirade and, shockingly, offered a few words of encouragement.

"It was obvious he was trying to bait you into a confrontation with an audience. You handled that very well."

I was livid over the entire incident. Something as trivial as a mailbox just got turned into a full-blown controversy. I had expected no less of Mike, but I had expected a little more from the supervisors.

Needless to say, I went to the captain about it. His response to a female officer getting called a bitch and a cunt in a squad room full of officers and supervisors was, "You can't have a hissy fit every time someone calls you a name!"

AFTER THAT, THE SITUATION grew much worse—the wolf pack had officially designated me as their target. Although I had tried to steel myself, nothing prepared me for what lie ahead. Most nights, I would take my time getting ready for work in the locker room so I wouldn't run into any of the pack from the second shift, Mike and Brad included. I would walk into roll call at precisely eleven p.m. My own shift wasn't so bad; I had a few supporters, and the others just wanted to stay out of it all.

It became a weekly occurrence that I would come to work to find my name blacked out all over the department: union board, cruiser assignment sheets, mailbox, extra security details I had signed up for. Someone had gone around with a black Magic Marker and crossed my name out of existence. I thought it was pretty juvenile, but then could I possibly expect more from the Harrises?

The last week of December 2002, I left the locker room and began walking down the hallway where Brad Harris stood, waiting. Upon seeing me, he started walking directly toward me. When we got to the point of passing each other, I stepped as far to the right as I could, but Brad did, too. Using his shoulder, he sent me flying into the wall—a full-blown body check. I stood there in shock as he smiled and walked away. He knew I hadn't been coming to roll call until precisely eleven p.m. Everyone else had either gone home or was seated in the squad room, which was why he'd waited until then to do it—no witnesses. It was all I could do to maintain my composure for the next eight hours until I could go home. By that point, I was physically sick driving to work every night, not knowing what to expect when I got there.

Of course, when I tried to explain the incident to the captain, he simply changed subjects and didn't even acknowledge what I had said.

There was a lot of overtime that had to be worked at the department, so I faced the possibility of having one of the wolf pack members on my shift for a few hours. I didn't care too much about the others, since they were just followers, but I put in a request to my sergeant that if Mike or Brad worked over on the night shift, to please put us in separate zones. He happily granted the request since he had been conscious of what was going on. Although he did his best to support me, he really didn't have many options. He knew that if he went to the captain, he would be wasting his time, and there was nothing else he could do.

For the next six months, I escaped any further physical abuse, but the juvenile harassment continued. Once in a while I fought back—nothing major, like the time I had to sit in front of Brad in the squad room. I had perfume on, and he started waving his hand in front of his face.

"Good God, something sure fucking stinks in here!" he said, referring to me.

"It's probably your breath," I said without missing a beat. "You should brush your teeth more than once a month, you know."

"Fuck off," was his only response.

I smiled.

They tried simple intimidation tactics. For instance, when

I sat in the squad room alone, Brad would come in, sit in the chair next to me, and move it as close as he could without touching. Then he would sit there and stare at the wall. If I was behind him while we were walking into the department, he would wait until I got close before slamming the door in my face. By the end of January 2003, they upped it a notch and started to compromise my safety on the street. If any of them worked over on my shift, they would key their cruiser microphones anytime I tried to talk. If I tried to tell the dispatcher where I was or what I was doing, they'd key up their own radio mics and my transmission wouldn't go through. I shuddered to think what would happen if I had to call for help. My own supervisors were pissed, but there was nothing they could do, although they tried to talk to the captain. He gave his usual response: "You can't prove who's doing it! Just let it go!"

Believe it or not, I did have a significant ally in the department: Detective Sergeant Frank Anthony, a longtime veteran and pivotal force at Mayberry. Known for his investigative skills, he performed all the internal investigations and major cases. Most important, no one messed with him and he had no qualms about speaking his opinions. Even the wolf pack knew better than to go against Frank. He was intimidated by no one (or so I believed for many years) and took me under his wing when I was first hired—he was my department mentor. When things began to heat up with the pack and me, he'd frequently walk into the squad room and tell the entire second shift, "You guys keep your shit up with Stacy and you're gonna find yourself in a major jam!" They'd laugh at him, and he finally approached me and said, "You are putting up with entirely too much shit around here."

Surprisingly, I found a small ally in, of all people, Lieutenant Roberts—how ironic. It wasn't about me, though. He absolutely hated the administration and took any opportunity to bring them down or watch them squirm. That included being nice to me and telling me on a daily basis that I needed to get an attorney and sue the department for harassment. I could only raise an eyebrow and shake my head at him, knowing he had been one of the worst offenders for years.

By May 2003, knowing they would never be disciplined, the pack became so blatant in their harassment that it was a downright joke. It was all I could do at that point to even go to work. I was having a horrible time sleeping, and I was as stressed as I could get.

I started finding my department mailbox in disarray. Someone had been going through it, and certain court subpoenas were missing. Every day, subpoenas were put in our mailboxes informing us of a date and time to appear in court. By the time I arrived at work, they were gone. It was only after I missed my first court appearance that I realized what was happening. The city prosecutor assured me the subpoena had been issued and put inside my mailbox. With this malicious act, the pack had gone criminal, in my opinion. If an officer missed court one time too many, he or she faced termination in addition to possible contempt of court charges.

My supervisors told me to take up the matter with the captain. I could only assume that with a situation as serious as court subpoenas, he might actually do something about it.

"You have no expectation of privacy with department mailboxes," he said rudely.

"Um, okay, but they're taking my court subpoenas."

"You'll have to prove it!"

As I began walking out of his office, I couldn't help airing my grievances: "I've had just about enough of this shit as I'm going to take."

I figured he would call me back in and threaten me with insubordination, but that would have required him to do his job. Therefore he remained silent.

I could have gone to the chief, but his programmed response was, "Take it up with the captain." He couldn't possibly risk missing a minute of the daily talk shows.

By then, the attacks were coming so frequently that I would walk through the department door with my jaw clenched, not knowing what to expect. I had prepared myself to walk in and find out they had issued an arrest warrant on me for some trumped-up charge. Before I went home every morning, I had to "rig" my locker so I could tell if someone was getting in it during the day. And they were. Every night before I went out on the street, I had to thoroughly search my assigned cruiser for tape recorders, drugs, or anything else I could think of that they could have put in there to get me in trouble. And I was followed to every call I responded to by "persons unknown."

The union issues were getting ready to blow up as well. A few officers were toying with the idea of working twelve-hour shifts, so I hung up a notice asking for everyone's thoughts on the matter. If they didn't like it, so be it. Again, I was accused of using the union for personal gain, which made no sense to me at all. I couldn't understand how switching unions and working different hours benefited me. Also, the officers who broached the idea of switching unions were claiming I gave them "inaccurate" information and jumped on the wolf pack bandwagon. Still, we set up a meeting for June 13, 2003, to discuss the issue.

On the sidelines, Lolita and the wolf pack had joined forces. I wasn't aware of it then, but I was about to be very soon.

As difficult as it was, I have to say that I was proud of the fact that I didn't back down. Most officers who were targets of the wolf pack never lasted this long; they usually quit after a month or two. In my situation, the more they pushed, the more I fought back. They looked for anything they could to get me in trouble or confront me with, but I dotted all my i's and crossed my t's. So what was the only thing they could find to taunt me with? I smoked cigarettes—a truly heinous crime!

I was up for a position as a field training officer, and the captain bypassed me. Ignoring my years of experience and training, he picked an officer who had been on the department for only two years. His reason was that I smoked and set a horrible example for younger officers. When I tried to explain that I didn't drive around for eight hours with a cigarette hanging out of my mouth, he said, "It doesn't matter." Several other officers smoked, but again, this was the only card they could play with me, so they used it.

On May 24, 2003—less than a month before the union meeting—I came to work to find "PIG STY" written on the cruiser board underneath my cruiser number. I shared my cruiser with two other officers and made a conscious effort to keep it spotless. I already knew it was something they could use against me, so I didn't want to give them any ammunition. Apparently, it didn't matter; they just made it up anyway. The next night, a sticker was placed under my cruiser number with my badge number written on the board (in case I didn't realize the sticker was intended for me!). The sticker said, "Is this a hog pen or a four-wheeled ashtray?—Anonymous."

The wolf pack sergeant simply couldn't ignore this (I'm pretty sure that was the point of the sticker), so he went out and inspected my cruiser. He wrote up a memo that read, "Very dirty inside. Shotgun is rusty/dirty. Needs immediate attention. Windows yellow from smoke haze." They continued to rip me to shreds the next day, and my sergeant overheard them. Since the focus of their comments was my cruiser, he decided to have a look for himself. After he realized it was bullshit, he did his best to defend me in a memo to the shift lieutenant.

After Officer Dittrich complained about the harassment and Lieutenant Phillips described the condition he found the shotgun in as horrible, I decided to do some research. Sgt. Price wrote in his cruiser inspection...(noted above) I did an immediate inspection afterward and the only problem I found was that ½ quart of oil was needed and the floor could use a vacuuming. The line for the shotgun was marked, so apparently had passed inspection BY Lieutenant Phillips....This cruiser was not close to being as bad as described by the second shift supervisors....

As you already know from our prior conversations, I was never made aware of any problems concerning Officer Dittrich's cruiser. I spoke to the other shift supervisors whose officers share the cruiser with Dittrich, and none of them recall ever being contacted by Sgt. Price about the cruiser needing "immediate attention."

Just more trivial garbage to rattle my chains. And it didn't take a genius to figure out that the memo and stickers were ignored by the administration. It may not seem like much, but to experience this type of thing day after day wears you down, emotionally and physically. I grew very tired of having to defend myself. There were many days that I felt like throwing in the towel, but I had two little girls to take care of, and I would not make them suffer financially because of a group of thugs.

I had already contacted an attorney in Cleveland who vowed to "drain that cornpoke town dry" after she'd seen the documents and heard the tapes. Strangely, I was still afraid of becoming that stereotype they'd expected me to be when I got hired. If I filed a lawsuit, it would be a department-wide "See—told you so! This happens every time a female officer gets hired!" It's amazing that after all of this I would actually care what anyone thought, but I did. Most important, if I were ever to try to get hired at another police department, the lawsuit would undoubtedly come into play. Bottom line was, if I filed a lawsuit, my career as a police officer would be over. Furthermore, the attorney informed me that once the suit was filed things would get much, much, worse, and I would probably have to quit if I wanted to maintain a shred of sanity. I felt defeated and angry. I loved being a police officer and had looked forward to this since I was a child. Now I faced the possibility of having it all taken away by a group of juvenile assholes and a spineless administration. It didn't seem fair.

On June 4, 2003, I took a step that seemed to be my last option outside of a lawsuit. Escorted by another union representative and my sergeant, I handed Captain Salsgiver a formal complaint for harassment on the job and a hostile work environment. Brad Harris had filed the same complaint against Nathan Fultz, so I figured the captain would "get it." It specifically named Brad and Mike Harris and their two supervisors, Sergeant Price and Lieutenant Phillips. I was forcing the administration's hand, but it still gave them a little wiggle room.

The captain became completely unglued.

He started shaking the complaint at me, ranting and raving. He went so far as to say, "You better expect to get the cold shoulder after this! You know how it is, and don't act surprised when it happens!" We all just sat there shaking our heads at him, figuring he'd be smart enough to realize we were tape-recording the conversation. He wasn't. He didn't even calm down enough to look at the complaint. Yet after all of this, I still made it easy for him. (Although looking back, I wished I hadn't.) I wasn't asking for a full-blown investigation. I wrote:

When I come to work and have to deal with hostility such as this, it makes it increasingly difficult to perform my duties. I have made several attempts to have this matter taken care of informally; however, it has continued. The only adjustment I request is that the order is conveyed to the named officers and supervisors—in a serious manner, to cease their behavior immediately. I expect absolutely no repercussions from this complaint and I simply want to be left alone to do my job.

In layman's terms, I asked the captain to do his job and tell them to knock their shit off, period. He didn't see it that way and essentially threw us out of his office. When I went home and told Rich about the meeting, he wasn't surprised.

"You're beating a dead horse," he told me. "You know they'll do absolutely nothing about it, and it's only going to get worse. You need to get out of that hellhole!"

We both knew I needed the job, but it was frustrating to both of us. I knew there were times he was downright furious but felt helpless. I dreaded going to work that night and slept very little during the day. I couldn't imagine what waited for me.

I didn't think things could get much worse, but I was seriously mistaken.

When I arrived at work that night, I had basically just walked through the door when I heard the pack inside the squad room, laughing. They were joking about the "Salsgiver ass chewing" they had received earlier. So much for the "convey in a serious manner" written in my complaint. It was a total joke.

The next morning after my shift was over, the captain

called me and the union representative back into his office. He gave a half-ass apology for the way he had acted the day before but proceeded to tell me, "Just so you know, this complaint is public record, so anyone can see it."

"So?" I wondered what his point was.

"Well, I'm just telling you."

Then I understood: A subtle threat hid behind his words. Basically, he was telling me that he could release my letter to anyone he wanted to and it would make *me* look bad. He further informed me that he'd instructed Sergeant Price and Lieutenant Phillips to speak to the Harrises and tell all of them to stop.

"Oh, they 'instructed' them all right," I said. "They were laughing their asses off about it in roll call last night. Are you going to ask them *why* they're acting this way? I can't imagine they'd go this far over the Nathan Fultz incident unless there's something else I don't know about." I knew I was wasting my time.

"No! You just wanted them to stop, that's all!" he said defensively.

"I just assumed—as a captain of a police department—you might want to get to the root of the problem to ensure something like this doesn't happen again."

"I can't say a word to them because of the union!" This was total bullshit. "And furthermore, if you don't want someone rifling through your department drawer or mailbox, don't keep important papers in there!"

I was furious. "Or you could just handle the problem!"

"I'm done." He waved me off.

"I'm not! I'm concerned about having these two work over-time on my shift. They won't back me up if needed, and it's an issue of safety!"

"Has that happened yet?"

"No, but—"

"Then it's not even an issue!" he cut me off.

"Unbelievable," I muttered as I walked out of his office.

The union representative stayed behind and talked to the captain further. He learned that the captain took my complaint to every supervisor and basically said, "See what she did!" The representative questioned his motives, and the captain told him that any complaint filed was public record, so he could do whatever he wanted. He further told him that he'd instructed every supervisor to "not let this complaint get in the way of doing your job. If Officer Dittrich does something wrong, make sure you discipline her for it as you see fit."

The captain waged his own battle with me at that point. Just five days after I filed the complaint, the union rep approached me.

"Got some bad news for you," he began.

My stomach immediately started churning, a feeling I had grown accustomed to. *Now what?* my head screamed.

"As soon as you filed the complaint, Brad went to the captain and asked if he could change his shift to midwatch...."

"That means he would be working with me for four hours! Don't tell me—"

"The captain granted his request."

"It's outside of the shift-bidding schedule! That totally violates the union contract!"

In all my years there, no one had ever been allowed to switch his shift in the middle of a cycle unless there was a dire family emergency or extenuating circumstances.

"The captain signed off on it without blinking an eye," he told me. "The only reason Brad wants to work midwatch is to fuck with you, and this really should've opened their eyes to it, but it didn't. That tells me the captain *wants* him to fuck with you....You really should get an attorney."

All I could do was sigh.

My supervisors went to the captain immediately and stated they were vehemently opposed to Brad coming to the shift, and why would he allow it?

"If they can't get along outside of work, fine. But they better get along here, and if you see a problem, you better handle it!" he barked at them.

As the date for the union meeting approached, I was still finding my name blacked out everywhere, and my locker and mailbox had been gone through. One night, I was passing by Lieutenant Phillips's office and overheard him telling a new probationary officer that if he got involved in union issues or voiced support for the union switch, he might not make it through probation. I flipped.

"What are you doing?" I stuck my head inside the door. "Did you seriously just threaten a probationary officer? You can't do that!"

"Get the fuck out!"

I notified the other union representatives, and they were equally pissed. They stated that what he'd done was a complete violation of union standards, and an unfair labor practice suit could be filed against the city because of it. This time, we alerted the chief first. When faced with a possible suit by the police union, the chief shut off his television and took action for the first time in years. He laid into Lieutenant Phillips and threatened him with disciplinary action if he did it again. Of course, Lieutenant Phillips focused his outrage solely on me. This time, I didn't care, since he was the one who'd taken part in, and enabled, the harassment. Finally, the tables had been turned, if only for one day. The day after his ass chewing, I passed him in the hallway.

"You owe me an apology!" he grumbled.

"Are you serious? After everything you and your cronies have put me through, you want *me* to apologize? I find that downright humorous, and don't hold your breath." I walked away.

THE TENSION IN THE air the day of the union meeting was so thick, it would have taken a chain saw to cut through it. People were grumbling at one another, but for the most part, they were grumbling about me. Right before the meeting, I went into the locker room and found Lolita in there. Up until then, she had been nice to my face but kept her distance (or so I thought). However, I had my suspicions.

"I'm not gonna let these guys rip you to shreds in there! Don't let them beat you down!" she said supportively.

We walked into the meeting, and it was so quiet that you

could hear a pin drop. I was seated at the union table with the two other reps and the union attorney. When it was asked who would start the meeting, Lolita raised her hand.

"I want to know why Stacy purposely misled us with the union information and sign-up cards," she said calmly.

My jaw dropped to the floor. Lolita had waited for the right moment, when all her followers were together, to strike out at me. She had even set me up for it by pretending to be friends just minutes prior.

As soon as she made her statement, the room exploded (mainly members of the wolf pack, which had grown to almost ten people by then). They were screaming at me that everything was all about my own gain. The other union reps were trying to deflect their comments, saying it was impossible for me to gain any more than another union member, but their efforts were fruitless.

Lolita was leading the pack, and I decided to let it all out. At that point, I felt I didn't have much to lose.

"I'd like to know how you're aware of anything that goes on around here since you seem to be wrapped up in your own extracurricular activities on duty!" I yelled out.

It had gotten so bad that we were both standing, almost in a face-off, with a few officers in between. Her eyes widened and her face turned red at my accusation. Kevin Morgan, intelligently, didn't say a word.

"I don't know what you're talking about!" she snapped.

"Really? If you don't want to open that can of worms, honey, then sit down and shut up!"

She actually started to come at me, and I laughed. "Oh, please, good luck with that, sweetie."

Her followers blocked her and tried to calm her down while I fended off other attacks—horrible and nasty personal attacks that had nothing to do with union issues. By then, I had lost my composure to the point where I felt like throwing chairs. Obviously, the meeting ended abruptly and nothing was accomplished as far as the union was concerned. The only useful thing that came out of it was my discovery that Lolita had been behind a lot of what had been happening over the last six months.

I walked straight out of the department without talking to anyone and drove home. When I walked in the front door, I lost it. Everything that had happened to me over the past several months came to a head, and I felt I simply couldn't take it anymore. As I sat on the floor sobbing, I played the tape of the meeting, which I had secretly recorded, for Rich. He was furious.

"This is bullshit. I don't want you working there anymore!" he cried, pacing around our kitchen. "This has gotten way out of hand—what a bunch of assholes....I'm serious, I want you to quit!"

"I'm not quitting!" I protested. "I worked hard for this job, and I'm not leaving!"

"You better be careful, then. You know how they are—they're going to go after you full throttle after this. I'm just worried they're going to try to stick something criminal on you. They've done it before."

I didn't sleep all day and went to work that night for four hours before going home sick. The next morning, the hits kept coming. The other union rep called me and said he'd been cornered by the wolf pack (Lolita and her lover, Kevin, included). They wanted me to step down as union director. Since they didn't represent the union majority, I refused. On a positive note, he informed me that the veteran day shift officers had been disgusted by the meeting and now realized that the pack was using the union to further their vendetta against me.

That night at work, Lieutenant Roberts told me he'd actually confronted the chief and captain in the hallway. He'd told them he was getting sick and tired of hearing the Harrises mouthing off about me the minute they walked in the door—it was getting old, and they were nothing but a constant problem within the department. He further told them they were both out of their minds to allow Brad Harris to work the same shift with me. For a twenty-four-hour period, I was actually starting to feel a sense of support from the majority.

But, as always, the worst was yet to come.

On June 15, 2003—two days after the blowout—I responded to an injury accident on the north side of the city. It wasn't my zone, but it sounded pretty bad. I was the fourth officer to arrive on the scene. The fire department had to pull the driver out of his car and told us he was completely "shit-faced" (drunk).

There's a phenomenal amount of paperwork involved in reporting a DUI (driving under the influence) crash, so it's always been standard practice that one officer handles the DUI paperwork while another handles the crash report. I had been on the scene for about twenty minutes when I found that the other officers had gone, leaving me to handle all the paperwork. And it wasn't even my zone! I could've called them back and complained, but the last thing I needed was problems with my own shift.

When an officer is about to make a DUI arrest, state law requires that he or she read the driver pertinent information from the administrative license suspension (ALS) form, which outlines the consequences of taking (or refusing to take) a chemical (blood, breath, or in some cases urine) test. The driver needs to sign the form, acknowledging that the information had been read to him by the arresting officer. At that point, the arresting officer is required to administer the test within two hours, which is the window of opportunity for accurately determining an individual's blood alcohol level.

In this particular case, the driver was in and out of consciousness and was promptly transported to the hospital. I drove to the department and grabbed a blood-testing kit, since it was clear the driver would never be able to take a Breathalyzer test. When I arrived at the hospital, the driver was in a CAT scan tube and undergoing numerous tests. I told the attending physician I needed to speak to the driver in a timely manner and would he please call me as soon as they were through. He assured me he would.

I left the hospital and pulled into a nearby empty parking lot, where I began the ungodly amount of paperwork. I sat there for several hours, having the dispatcher call the hospital to check the status of the driver. A few officers stopped by, asked if I wanted any help, gabbed a bit, and moved on. The two-hour time frame had passed, but I wasn't too worried about it. The hospital had gotten the driver to sign a medical release form that included all requisite bloodwork. He might not ultimately be charged under an administrative license suspension, but he could still be charged with DUI. After I served the man all of his paperwork, I went back to the parking lot and finished it.

Frank Anthony was filling in that night for my sergeant. He checked my report, approved it, and signed off on it.

On June 19, 2003, Lieutenant Roberts told me that during a staff meeting that day, there had been some grumblings about a certain "female officer" gabbing after a DUI report and screwing up the paperwork. I figured it was one of the second shift supervisors trying to stir things up again.

I saw Frank the next night and asked him if he'd heard what was said.

"Don't say anything more." He put up his hand, looking angry. "We're going to discuss it after your roll call; I have the paperwork ready to go in my office."

I was stunned and confused.

After roll call, Lieutenant Roberts and I walked into Frank's office and sat down before he turned on his tape recorder. I had my own running as well. My head was spinning as I tried to figure out what I had done wrong.

"Tell me about the DUI/crash," he began.

"Is this a disciplinary meeting? Do I need a union rep?" I was sweating and starting to freak out. I had never seen Frank so formal.

"I don't know yet!" he barked. "I want to hear what you have to say! Your job performance on this DUI/crash is very poor and substandard."

He pointed to an extremely minor mistake on the crash report. Instead of writing the number 2, which meant the accident involved an injury, I had written the number 3, which meant "property damage only."

He continued, "Your times are off, too. I checked the log."

"Those are the times the dispatcher gave me over the radio," I interjected.

"What you did here was write false information on a report—that's a crime."

Finally, I understood what was happening.

"What are you doing, Frank?" I said quietly. "What is this?"

"I'm investigating a complaint—"

"That's bullshit and you know it! You've got to be kidding me that this is the best they can come up with...and they dragged you into it." I shook my head. "I thought you were above this kind of crap."

"You were sitting around parking lots gabbing all night instead of doing your job, and then tried to cover your ass," he countered.

"Oh, I get it now." I was shaking. "They ordered you to do this, right? You do an investigation, get me charged with a crime, and then I'm thrown out on my ass, which is exactly what they want. Am I right? Am I right?"

"You're right that I think something else is going on around here. You're obviously preoccupied, and it's affecting your job—"

"Thank you, I couldn't have said it better myself," I interrupted.

He ignored me. "You better talk to someone about what's going on, so let's hear it—out with it."

I was pretty sure this whole thing was a front and an ultimatum. The administration was worried that I had gotten my own attorney and wanted to get a jump on things. They wanted Frank to get that information from me since they knew we were close—and if he didn't, they would threaten me with a crime. It also dawned on me that Lolita had been in the detective bureau now for two weeks, working side by side with Frank. Whatever she had done, or whatever she had said to him, apparently worked. Sitting in that office I had encountered my worst fear. It was what I'd been afraid of all along.

"I don't think this is the appropriate place to discuss what's going on with me personally. It's my understanding we're here to talk about my 'poor and substandard' report," I challenged.

"I know it's been a long time since I've done a DUI, but I know it sure as hell doesn't take *that* long!"

I reminded him that there was a crash involved, and I had handled the entire report alone. I asked him if he had spoken to the officers who had pulled up to me that night. They could certainly attest to the fact that I was doing paperwork. When I learned that he hadn't even bothered to talk to them, I was further convinced the entire "investigation" was a setup. When he asked why the ALS form hadn't been read to the driver within the two-hour period, I explained that it was a little difficult to do that when someone was in a CAT scan tube.

"Why didn't you read it to him when he was in back of the ambulance?"

"Because he was in there unconscious with his head split open," I said sarcastically.

He kept throwing question after question at me, all ridiculous, and I finally pointed out the obvious:

"I hate to remind you that you are the one that checked the report and signed off on it. Apparently, at the time you thought it was fine."

"I don't know much about DUIs and that crap until it was pointed out to me," he countered.

The more questions I answered, the more uncomfortable he grew. He knew it was all a charade, but he had most likely been ordered by the administration to handle it this way. My answer to his final question provided a major blow to his trumped-up accusations.

"You never even attached the medical release form to your paperwork!"

"I certainly did. It was attached to the ticket itself and filed with the court," I said calmly.

"*They* didn't give that to me." He paused, sighing. "Things are starting to make a little more sense now."

I wanted to scream, *Aw, c'mon, Frank! You mean you're not in on the joke?*

He actually had a written reprimand ready to go for "lacking competency," but in the end he tossed it in the garbage. I could tell he was fighting his own battle between doing what was right and doing his job. But I knew it wasn't over. The administration would not be happy with Frank's action and would order him to continue with the investigation. When I left Frank's office, I went directly into the locker room and vomited—I was that upset. Frank had been the one person I could always count on. But now, perhaps because of pressure from the administration, he had turned on me. I lost respect for him, and that upset me more than everything else combined.

When I left the department, it was all I could do even to drive. I pulled over and called Rich, hysterical. He had known Frank a lot longer than I had, and they were friends. Like me, Rich was in shock.

"I knew something like this was going to happen, I just can't believe Frank was the one to do it. They had to have ordered him, he would never do something like this on his own."

"He did it, plain and simple! Ordered or not, this is down-right criminal!" I was almost hyperventilating and began to get sick to my stomach all over again.

If I'd had an ounce of trust in the prosecutors I knew, I wouldn't have worried too much; any competent prosecutor would have laughed at the department's claims of my "falsi-fying a report." But Frank had a lot of pull with them. Any-thing he turned in, they approved without question. To make matters worse, I still had an entire eight-hour shift to work; I would have to be on my game, diligent and aware, cautious and safe.

Somehow I made it through my shift and went home to take on the grueling task of gathering a defense for myself. Obviously, I didn't sleep. I called the dispatch center and asked them to pull the radio traffic of the DUI/crash. They did and played it to me. I was right: The dispatcher had given me the wrong times. I asked them to record the traffic on tape, and I'd pick it up on my shift. After that, I called the records department and had them pull the last twenty crash reports filed by various officers and place copies in my mailbox.

When I got to work that night, the crash reports were there, along with a note from Frank. It read, "You're not getting the tape from dispatch." At least he was now aware that the times I'd given had been provided by the dispatchers—not that it mattered at this point.

I went through the crash reports and highlighted far worse mistakes than mine on every single one of them, times included. Several of the reports were from supervisors as well. I made copies with the highlights and placed them in Frank's mailbox. I didn't need to write anything; he'd understand. Basically, I was saying, "If you're going to discipline me for this, you'd better sharpen your pencil, because there's a hell of a lot of officers doing the same thing."

A few days after that, I was approached by one of the city prosecutors who happened to be on the up-and-up. He was a good guy.

"What the hell is going on at your department? I heard the entire buzz about that DUI crap and told Frank what he's doing is ridiculous. The guy already pleaded guilty to the DUI!"

"I don't even want to discuss it," I told him, knowing that if Frank filed charges against me, it certainly wouldn't be with him.

"Sounds like it's a damn circus over there," he muttered as he walked away.

The days during that investigation felt like months. I didn't sleep or eat. Mostly I cried. Rich was a wreck; he worried horribly every night I'd walk out the door to go to work, wondering if that would be the night I got arrested or got hurt because I had no backup.

After all the waiting, I went to work one night and was called immediately to Frank's office. I gave a quick call to Rich, telling him that if he didn't hear from me, that meant I was probably in jail and to call an attorney. I remember walking down the hallway in a daze, positive the end was coming. I was thinking, *All of this because I wrote a wrong number and wrote times given to me by the dispatchers.* But I knew it was more than that: It was a battle of egos and a blatant display of disrespect and contempt that had gone on the better part of a year. It was downright wrong, and I knew at that point there wasn't a damn thing I could do about it.

I stood outside Frank's office and took a deep breath. *All right,* I thought, *let's do this.*

I went in, and he got down to business. There would be no criminal charges, and he was giving me an oral reprimand for incompetence. An oral reprimand couldn't be grieved by the union, but it would still be placed in my file. Basically, I couldn't fight it.

Then he added a unique twist to the discipline: I had to write a few pages on the proper procedure of obtaining blood during a DUI arrest.

"What?"

"You heard me."

"That insinuates I didn't do a blood test properly, which you know wasn't the case."

"You're a good writer; write more than a few pages, and who knows, maybe you could get the damn thing published as an instruction manual," he said. Little did he know how prophetic that statement would turn out to be.

I didn't argue, just sat there in silence. I wasn't going to jail, and anything further would be a waste of my time. I signed off on the reprimand and had stood up to walk out when Frank offered his last words:

"You know, when you were back here as a detective, you were one of the best investigators I have ever seen.... Don't let things around here change you. I'd like to see that woman again someday."

I gave a sarcastic laugh. "I think it's safe to say at this point, Frank, that *that* woman is dead and was buried a long time ago."

Whether Frank had a "come to Jesus" meeting with himself, or whether the department decided they might be close to crossing the line with such a ridiculous charge, the reason the investigation ended with such a whimper no longer mattered. The damage was done and there would be no going back. Many years later, as I write this, the one thing about it all that still gnaws at me is what happened with Frank. I don't know that I'll ever get over it.

After I left Frank's office, I called Rich and gave him an

update. I had resigned myself to the fact that the abuse would never end. And he agreed. "It's time to call the attorney and file the suit," he told me. Even though this investigation was closed, another one would undoubtedly open at some point. Maybe not this week, but perhaps the week after that. I had lost the battle—my career as a police officer was officially over.

Not so fast.

Two days after my oral reprimand, a miracle occurred. Rich called me from work, and I could tell he was excited.

"Don't call the attorney yet! Richland County is hiring deputies, so you need to go there right now and see Lieutenant Kauffman to put your application in."

Richland County was my home and also home to Mansfield City, where my entire family worked at the Mansfield Police Department. Rich knew all the Richland County sheriff's deputies, and I don't know why it never dawned on me to apply there. The Mayberry Police Department thumbed their noses at Mansfield PD and Richland County—an area five times larger than Mayberry, with five times the amount of crime (the previous summer had seen twelve homicides within a three-month period).

I immediately put in my application with Lieutenant Eric Kauffman, dreading the question I knew was coming.

"Why do you want to leave Mayberry?" he asked.

Luckily, Mayberry wasn't exactly looked on favorably by other police departments, and the Harrises were disliked by most cops in the area. In addition, everyone at Richland County knew my family, so that would be a help. As I started to explain the reason for my desire to leave, Lieutenant Kauffman put up his hand.

"No need, I got it....I've heard plenty about that place, and I don't blame you for wanting to leave. We'll keep your background check under the radar, so to speak."

I was exhilarated, and for the first time in months, I actually believed I might be able to salvage what was left of my career. Even more ironic was the fact that people like Brad Harris had tried to get a job in Mansfield and failed—no one could stand him. Kevin Morgan actually got hired, but he quit and went back to Mayberry after he found out how dangerous the city was. Many of the officers who worked at Mayberry had grown up there, but I didn't—and I'd always felt like an outsider.

The day Lieutenant Kauffman called me and said, "Have at it, go turn your resignation in, you're hired," I felt as if a twenty-pound weight had been lifted off my shoulders. I can't say I was thrilled at having to start from the bottom again (no seniority), but it was worth it.

When I turned in my resignation at Mayberry, I expected to hear cheers of, "Thank God she's gone, we did it!" But, ironically, I didn't. A couple of jaws dropped since no one knew I had even applied elsewhere. The administration felt snubbed because Richland County had disregarded their reported opinion of me. And I was able to walk away with my head held high, beating the stereotype I had almost represented without compromising who I was. As far as I was concerned, I had beaten the wolf pack.

When I first started at Richland County, I was welcomed

with open arms and actually felt I was around my own "people." There was a camaraderie there that I had never experienced, a brotherhood that felt unbelievable. We all watched one another's backs, knowing the most important thing was to go home at night safe and sound. It was a breath of fresh air, and it enabled me to get back to what I enjoyed doing most—being a cop. Sure, there were ups and downs, as with everything else, but nothing that even came close to the horror I'd experienced at Mayberry PD.

ABOUT THREE YEARS after I began at Richland County, I was sent to Mayberry with another deputy. Mayberry was requesting assistance from other departments for an armed robbery where the gunmen were holed up. I dreaded going there. I had not stepped foot within the city limits since the day I'd left.

As it turned out, the gunmen weren't holed up by the time I arrived, so I was free to leave. As I was pulling away from the scene, I saw a Mayberry officer approaching my car. It was Kevin Morgan. Preparing myself for a confrontation, I rolled down my window. What he said shocked me.

"I know this is a little late coming, and you probably don't want to hear a word I have to say, but I'm really sorry for everything we put you through," he said, looking uncomfortable. "You were right about Lolita, the union, the whole mess—and you didn't deserve any of that."

All I could do was look at him and nod. As he began to walk away, I was able to squeeze out a barely audible, "Thanks, Kevin."

Driving away from the scene, I was flooded with mixed emotions. A large part of me was angry, maybe because I couldn't help wondering if things might have ended differently if I'd handled the situation some other way. Kevin's apology essentially confirmed that none of it had been my fault. Mayberry subsequently had switched police unions and gone to twelve-hour shifts a year after I left—go figure. I did give Kevin a lot of credit for approaching me and apologizing after all this time. The other pack members, I knew, would never admit it if they felt the same way.

As I got on the highway to drive back, I felt the same sense of relief I'd felt the day I left Mayberry. I didn't belong there. I was going back to the place I belonged, in Richland County—I was headed home.

CHAPTER 13

The Judge Is God; the Prosecutor Is Jesus

I'VE HAD THE GOOD (and sometimes bad) fortune to work with many different prosecutors over the course of my career. I've dealt with several who had the public's interest at heart and truly wanted to see justice served. But I've also worked with prosecutors who were driven by ego and personal ambition—self-promoters who were a nightmare not only for law enforcement, but for the public as well. Once in a great while, the public catches on to this particular type and he or she won't get reelected, but for the most part the public doesn't see what goes on behind closed doors—and it's frightening, to say the least.

Most people tend to blame the judges and cops when a case goes awry, but many (although not all) miscarriages of justice are the result of self-interested prosecutors looking to advance their careers. The prosecutors decide whether or not to take a case to begin with, long before it makes its way to a judge. They weigh all the evidence, witness statements, and confessions to determine if a conviction is likely. You see, many prosecutors are so focused on their "conviction rate" that if there's a chance of a hung jury or a not guilty verdict, they'll reject the case rather than face a loss in the courtroom. Other times, they'll offer the defense a plea deal that waives jail time just so they can secure a recorded conviction. A genuinely caring prosecutor gets approval from the victim or the victim's family before offering a deal, but some prosecutors offer such deals to the defense without consultation, as long as it will enable them to strut their stuff before their peers and the community, boasting, "I have a one hundred percent conviction rate; nothing gets past me."

My first experience going "nose to nose" with this kind of prosecutor set the stage for my distaste for years to come.

I was investigating a report of child neglect and possible abuse in a run-down area of the city. When I walked into the home, I found two small children—a boy and a girl—sitting together in a stained old recliner. Next to them was a three-day-old bucket of cockroach-infested Kentucky Fried Chicken out of which they had been eating. Their parents (their mother and her boyfriend) were out at a restaurant eating dinner when we arrived.

There was very little furniture in the main room, which exposed the tattered, dog-feces-covered carpeting. A handful of fully covered fly catchers hung from the ceiling, with piles of flies underneath. Inside the kitchen, the countertops were covered with half an inch of old grease while gnats and other bugs swarmed around. The floor was covered with garbage, and there was little more than spoiled milk and a few cans of beer in the refrigerator. There was no electricity and no plumbing; the family was using their upstairs bathtub as a makeshift toilet. And the smell was unbearable.

When I spoke to the little girl, she indicated that she was being forced to perform oral sex on her mother's boyfriend and that both of the kids had been forced to smoke marijuana on several occasions. Because we had the authority to remove the children immediately, we summoned a county Child Protective Services worker and placed them in the custody of their grandmother, pending an investigation.

I had been on the force in Mayberry a little over a year at that point, and this was one of the most extensive investigations involving children I had handled up until then. I spent hours on the case, making sure my reports were detailed and perfect. I would have to appear in front of the juvenile court judge for a "shelter care" hearing and testify to my probable cause in removing the children. Most important, as a mother I was incensed at the thought of what these children had gone through, and I wanted their parents to be punished.

I arrived at the hearing fully prepared and eager to see the case through. I met with an assistant prosecutor I had never worked with before and was astonished at his passivity toward the case as a whole. He was standing in the hallway talking to numerous people about other cases and briefly pulled me to the side, asking questions that had clearly been answered in my report. After a few minutes of conversation, it dawned on me that he hadn't even read the damn thing. His information was coming strictly from the CPS caseworker. He was even unaware of the sexual assault allegations and drug use. He had planned to enter the courtroom to defend the rights of these children based only on a three-minute conversation he'd had with the caseworker. The hours of investigation and report writing that I'd poured into the case had been a waste.

Subsequently, when the hearing started the prosecutor gave a half-assed dissertation about the living conditions of the home that ended with, "Your Honor, I believe if we give the parents two weeks to improve the conditions, which includes electricity and running water, there shouldn't be a problem returning custody to them."

As he spoke, the caseworker sat there nodding. I had a look of shock on my face, which the judge must have noticed because he addressed me.

"Officer Dittrich, is there something you'd like to add?" he asked, smiling at me.

All eyes turned to me, and I felt my face burn as I stood up to answer him.

"Actually, Your Honor, there were other details in this case involving allegations of sexual and drug abuse that were clearly outlined in my report. I just feel that these allegations need to be investigated fully before the children are placed back with their parents."

"Duly noted, Officer. I order the caseworker from Child

Protective Services to investigate this matter and have her report to me when completed. In the future, I'd like to hear these details from the prosecutor without having to ask for them. Court adjourned."

Since the judge had just berated the prosecutor, I figured he'd be pissed, but I hadn't imagined it would be at me. Oh, how wrong I was!

We were barely in the hallway when I heard a voice behind me, getting louder by the second.

"Just who the fuck do you think you are? Don't you ever embarrass me in court again!" the prosecutor screamed at me.

"Embarrass you? He asked me a question! What was I supposed to do—ignore the judge?" I was trying to stay calmer than he was.

"You got a lot to learn, little girl! That is *my* courtroom in there, and you don't say a fucking word unless I tell you to!"

We were gathering a small crowd, and the caseworker stood there peering at me over her glasses and nodding in agreement with the prosecutor. At that point, I'd had enough. I didn't care who the guy was, I'd be damned if I was going to stand in a courthouse hallway and let him humiliate me that way.

"That's enough," I broke in, stopping him in midscream. "I'm done." And I turned to walk away.

This infuriated him further. "You're done? *You're done?* You're going to walk away from me, rookie?" he raved as I continued down the hallway.

By the time I got outside to my cruiser, I was shaking like a leaf, angry and upset. As I drove to the department, I kept going over and over the hearing, trying to figure out what I should've done differently. But it kept coming back to the one thing I couldn't ignore: No matter how important playing ball might be to this prosecutor's precious career, those children depended on me. The judge had asked me a question, and I had given him an honest answer.

The prosecutor apparently made a beeline for my department, because by the time I arrived, he had already been there and cornered one of the lieutenants in the parking lot. When I walked inside, the captain was already on the phone with the judge who'd presided over the hearing.

The judge completely sided with me—not that it mattered at that point, but at least it gave me a little peace of mind. He had heard about the commotion in the hallway shortly after it happened and he'd called my captain. He told him what had happened in the hearing, added that I had done absolutely nothing wrong, and said he intended to address the incident with the head county prosecutor.

Unfortunately for me, the judge wasn't calling the shots at this point. There was an underlying agreement between this prosecutor's office and my department: *You do what we say or you and your cases are fucked.* No one came out and said it in so many words, but that was the way it was. Things had been tense between the two agencies for a while, and as it turned out, I was about to become a sacrificial lamb.

The day after the incident, I was called into my captain's office and informed that he would be escorting me to a meeting at the prosecutor's office the next day.

"Why?" I barely managed to squeak out the word.

"Well, they just want to talk to you about proper court-room procedures," he said, looking uncomfortable.

"Um, it was my understanding that the judge said I didn't do anything wrong."

"This is just one of those things. I'll go with you, we'll listen to them complain and be done with it, that's all," he said.

That's all? I thought. I went home that night knowing sleep would be impossible. I spent hours waging a battle within myself over what was right and what I needed to do. I could have refused to attend the meeting, face disciplinary action, and get the union involved, but I had a baby girl to care for, and I didn't want to face the possibility of suspension. I couldn't afford to lose even a single day's pay. Therefore, I decided I'd go in and be done with it.

The captain's wife also happened to be a dispatcher, so when I walked into the department the day of the meeting, she informed me that the captain also hadn't slept, was nervous about the meeting, and truly wanted to get it over with. With my head screaming, *For Christ's sake! He's the captain, so why the hell are we going? Doesn't anyone have any balls around here?* I rode with the captain to the prosecutor's office.

I had envisioned that we would get called into the office of the head prosecutor, Rick Coffey, and sit there with the assistant prosecutor I'd had my incident with. I figured he would berate me for a few minutes, we'd all shake hands, and that would be the end of it.

Not even close.

I had rarely heard Rick Coffey's name without the word *asshole* attached to it. Having dealt with him only a few times in the past, I'd formed the opinion that he was extremely arrogant, but that was pretty much it. When the captain and I entered his office, *asshole* took on a whole new meaning. In the middle of his office were two chairs placed in the center of a circle of chairs—the "hot" seats. One was for me, the other for my captain; Rick pointed to them and gestured for us to sit down. After that, all the assistant prosecutors paraded in, each taking a designated seat in the circle around us. We faced Rick's desk, the entire setup resembling a nineteenth-century witch trial.

I had been tipped off by a fellow officer to secretly record the meeting in case of any further fallout, so as I took a deep breath, I reached up to my pocket to make sure the tape recorder was running smoothly. I noticed that my hand was shaking. Then the meeting started.

I think.

It basically began when Rick slowly clasped his hands together, put them on his desk, leaned forward, and glared at me. I looked around the circle and saw the other prosecutors doing the same thing. Believe it or not, this blatant intimidation went on for a good minute—a long time when you're waiting for the ax to fall. I remember thinking, *Are they serious? They actually get away with this crap?*

"We brought you in here, missy, to explain to you exactly what is expected from our law enforcement officers here," he began.

Ah, the deadly glare was over. Now we begin!

"Let me tell you that you are green—a rookie—and your holier-than-thou attitude won't be stood for around here...."

I glanced at the captain a couple of times in disbelief, mainly over the fact that he was sitting there not saying a word in my defense.

"I can assure you that your career here is going to be a very short one if you don't get with the program," Rick continued, his voice rising. "I can see by the look on your face that you're not taking me seriously!"

"I just don't appreciate being spoken to like a small child," I told him. "If there's something we can work out here—"

"I'm not finished! You sit there and listen!" he barked. "Your belligerence rose to the surface during the shelter care hearing, but I can assure you, ma'am, it will *not* be tolerated here!"

It was pointless to make even a small attempt at a defense. Their minds were made up, and this was simply a dog-and-pony show to make the assistant prosecutor (who had a smirk on his face the entire time) feel better. I began to stare at a pencil holder on his desk while he ranted and tuned him out. He ended the tirade with an order for the captain.

"I'm confident, Captain, that you are going to make sure this officer goes through extensive training as far as courtroom procedure goes?" he said sternly. "I'm sure the Peace Officer's Training Academy in London [Ohio] offers such classes?"

The captain nodded as I watched his balls roll out the door.

We left the meeting, and I literally could not speak to the captain. He tried to talk to me on the way back to the department, but all I could do was nod or shake my head. When I got into my own car to drive home, I was so angry, and there wasn't a damn thing I could do about it. I knew I had been thrown under the bus by my own people—the chief and captain in particular. My co-workers knew it, too. After the prosecutors' meeting, several supervisors cornered the chief, expressing their disdain at his decision to send me over there in the first place. According to one of them, he said, "Just admit it! You sent her over there as a sacrificial lamb, period!" They said the chief nodded in agreement and walked away from the bunch, flustered and with his head hung low. What a coward.

When I look back at that incident now, I can honestly say that if I had it to do all over again, I would never have said a word during that shelter care hearing. Why? Because two months later, those two children I had fought for were returned to their parents anyway. It simply wasn't worth the grief I went through.

This is a prime example of how one gradually loses compassion and ultimately develops a "why the hell should I care?" attitude. After this incident, I began to do my job in black and white: respond to a call, take the report, file charges, and move on to the next call. Whatever happened after that was out of my hands. Granted, after a few years I realized that this attitude was undermining my professionalism, and I snapped out of it—for a while.

But even so, from that point on my career would be an uphill battle. Every case or criminal charge I processed through the prosecutor's office was scrutinized and thrown out if it wasn't perfect. Not only that, but once the prosecutors alerted the local defense attorneys and court employees to the incident, I officially experienced my first round of being black-balled. Whenever I entered the courthouses, I was subjected to smirks and glares by various people. For years, several of the assistant prosecutors took small opportunities here and there to take pot shots at me.

For instance, there was the time I had been the responding officer to a brutal stabbing in a bar that resulted in a foot pursuit after I located the suspect in the bar's parking lot. I had been on maternity leave for five weeks following the birth of my second daughter and had been back to work for less than a week. Obviously, since I'd just had a baby, I had put on weight—another golden opportunity for one of the prosecutors to embarrass me. During my testimony, the prosecutor was explaining to the jury how the foot pursuit began, after which she added her own flourish.

"Now, Officer Dittrich, did you actually catch the suspect?" she asked me.

"No, I did not. Officer Morgan did," I responded.

"Ladies and gentlemen of the jury, I'll have to clear something up here. Officer Dittrich just recently returned from maternity leave and obviously put some weight on, so she wasn't able to run as fast as usual. Isn't that right, Officer?" she said, smirking.

I was horrified. "That's right," I admitted quietly.

Ironically, they all came around a little when I was moved to the detective bureau. I put together ironclad cases that were tough to poke holes through. Some of these drew the attention of the media, so there was little they could do but move forward with them. One year, I had a stabbing case that was tried by Rick Coffey. This time, after court, he called my lieutenant to say what a stellar case I had put together and how impressed he was with my testimony. I should have felt somewhat vindicated, but I could never forget the way they'd treated me in the beginning. Sure, I'd learned how to play the game as well as anyone else. I'd smile, be nice and professional, and do my job, but those grievances remained filed away in the back of my mind.

The Mayberry County prosecutors ran the show and let everyone know it: the police, the city prosecutors, and the court employees. It's unfortunate that my initial experiences had been restricted to Mayberry's county prosecutors. In the beginning years of my career, I pretty much assumed that what I'd seen in Mayberry was typical—but when I transferred to Richland County, I got quite a shock. The Mansfield-Richland prosecutors were completely pro–law enforcement; they treated the cops like professionals and worked side by side with us for the sole purpose of carrying out justice. There were a handful of self-serving prosecutors, sure, but the majority were on the up-and-up—and that made me reprogram my attitude toward the criminal justice system, to acknowledge (happily) that Mayberry was the aberration while Mansfield offered a collaborative model beneficial to all.

Again, I want to emphasize that many prosecutors out there are good people who choose to forgo a six-figure salary to do what's best for humanity. I've focused on the bad ones because I want everyone to be aware that such people exist in our communities. And I'm not talking just about the veterans—some prosecutors fresh out of law school aren't much help, either.

I remember one incident that took place close to the end of my shift. I was anxious to go home, and I was looking at having the next two days off. I had been dispatched to a disturbance call with another officer. A woman was at home with her boyfriend when her ex-husband showed up drunk, mouthing off. It was no big deal, actually. The ex-husband lived a few doors down, so we had planned to knock on his door, tell him to sleep it off for the night, and go home.

The ex-husband lived in a "makeshift" apartment building, and we were having a hard time finding the front door. I located a steel spiral staircase that went up to a door twenty feet off the ground. The other officer and I were actually joking around because the staircase was so narrow, only one of us could go up at a time.

I went first. The landing in front of the door was only about two feet wide, so we both couldn't stand on it at the same time—the other officer had to wait on the steps just below me. As I knocked on the door, the officer and I were chatting about our plans for our days off. I was in mid-laugh when I saw the man (ex-husband) come around the corner of the hallway. What caught my attention was what he was holding in his hands.

It was a fully loaded Russian assault rifle—an AK-47—and he had it pointed right at my chest.

Obviously, I pulled my pistol out of its holster with the full intention of shooting the guy. The only problem was that in order to cover myself, I had to move to the side of the door—and from that position, there was no possibility of getting a shot off at him. It was maddening.

I yelled, "Sheriff's Department! Drop your weapon immediately!" The other officer was scrunched down on the spiral steps, screaming into his portable radio that we had a "man with a gun—officers in trouble!"

At last, the man dropped the rifle and put up his hands.

I was shaking with the rush of adrenaline and furious at the knowledge that this psychopath might have killed me. I promptly handcuffed the guy and took him to jail, charging him with a slew of felonies.

Imagine how I felt when a twenty-one-year-old assistant prosecutor, fresh out of law school, called to inform me that he would not be filing felony charges. I went ballistic.

"Are you *insane*?" I screamed. "Have you completely lost your fucking *mind*? This guy, this convicted felon, a *drunk* felon, points a weapon that is totally illegal for him to own—a *loaded* assault rifle—at two officers and you are not going to charge him?" I further added, "What if I'd shot the guy? Huh? What then?"

He coughed into the phone and said with a complete lack of confidence, "Well, that's irrelevant. You didn't, and he dropped his weapon when you ordered—he was in complete compliance with—"

I slammed the phone down, picked it up, and slammed it down again. Then I actually picked up the phone again with the intention of throwing it right through the window, but another officer stopped me.

This young prosecutor knew as much about the law as a first-year law student. He had no concept of case law or prior court rulings, yet as a county prosecutor he was tasked with ensuring the public's safety (not to mention my own well-being) and had the power to determine which cases justified time in court.

I realize I've focused a lot of attention on county prosecutors, and it's true that as an entity they wield a significant amount of authority in the law enforcement community. However, when it comes to justice—or the best interests of the public—it is the judges (most important, the common pleas court judges) who control life and death, incarceration or freedom, justice or injustice.

These men and women are society's lifeline, and I don't believe the common citizen realizes the power a county judge wields or the devastation he can bring down on a community. There are many fine, upstanding judges who strive every day to mete out justice to the best of their ability. But I have also known judges who abuse their office for personal reasons. And the sad fact is that most citizens have no idea they exist.

One judge in particular comes to mind, a public official who seemed bent on abusing his oath of office to further the rights of criminals. It sounds crazy, I know, but I believe the facts will bear me out.

My first experience with this judge, August Sebastian, involved a felony theft. The case was fairly cut-and-dried: I had a scumbag chop-shop owner from a nasty part of town accuse a former employee of stealing thousands of dollars' worth of tires. I tracked down the employee, who confessed and actually led me to the stolen tires. Pretty simple, right?

Not quite. During the investigation, the "victim" chop-shop owner was stopping fellow officers of mine and asking them if I was married or if I'd be willing to date him. Obviously, I had no intention of doing so, but he continued to leave countless voice mail messages for me at work, stating, "Please! Call me!"

When the trial began, the scumbag victim testified to the fact that he had been wrong to accuse his former employee; he now believed him to be innocent. He further testified that he had left me numerous voice mails to inform me of such, but I had ignored his calls. When I testified, I explained that the employee had clearly committed the theft and that his confession—coupled with the fact that he had led me to the stolen goods—confirmed his guilt.

In mid-testimony, I was cut off by Judge Sebastian, who ordered me to explain why I hadn't returned the victim's phone calls. I attempted to point to the testimony of the other officers regarding the victim's personal interest in me and give my opinion that the victim had been trying to get in touch only to ask me for a date. Judge Sebastian again interrupted, stating that what I was saying was "hearsay."

The hearing was a bench trial, which meant the judge decided the verdict. At the end of the testimony, he stated unequivocally that this was a "he said/she said" matter and that he could not find the defendant guilty. Basically, he said that a law enforcement officer's testimony was no different from (no more credible than) that of a suspect with a criminal record. I was offended, but that didn't matter to Judge Sebastian; I was nobody to him, and he clearly didn't like cops.

This became evident when a city police lieutenant's son was beaten to death by a bar bouncer outside a city bar shortly after my theft trial. A friend of the lieutenant's son had gotten into an altercation as they were leaving the bar, and the son tried to intervene. The bouncer, a black belt in karate, grabbed the lieutenant's son and beat him to death, crushing his skull in the process. He hung on for a while but ultimately died from his injuries.

The prosecutor in charge of the case agreed to a plea deal of felonious assault (as opposed to murder), with the assumption that the judge would throw the book at the suspect. When Judge Sebastian sentenced the suspect to only three years, with the possibility of parole after one year, the family was outraged. During the sentencing, the lieutenant and his wife were audibly upset. Judge Sebastian started to berate the grieving parents in front of the courtroom, going so far as to order them thrown out. He continued to yell at the couple that the suspect "wasn't a murderer! He wasn't convicted of murder!" It astonished everyone. This judge had been elected to look out for the victims, yet he was treating them as if they were criminals. It was horrifying.

The end result? Judge Sebastian released the suspect on "shock probation" after only six months in prison.

Judge Sebastian was probably most notorious for courtroom

leniency when it came to sex offenders. In one particular case, the trial of an elderly male who had confessed to molesting several young boys, he sentenced the man to nothing more than probation. The case sparked outrage within the community and garnered the attention of national media commentators like Bill O'Reilly. However, Judge Sebastian's solution was simply to disappear for two weeks on an impromptu vacation and ignore media requests. The case went away, but the victims remained— as did the judge. Along with everything else, Judge Sebastian was widely known for giving convicted felons "two weeks to get their affairs in order." Meaning: Once a violent felon was convicted, the judge would give him two weeks of freedom to find alternative custody for his children, get his finances in order, and basically live it up before he went to prison for the rest of his life. Unfortunately, some of these thugs used the time to commit more heinous, violent crimes before they checked into the iron hotel. One man who was given his two weeks walked into an adult video store and bashed in the head of the female clerk before stealing all the money. When the cops arrived, part of this woman's brain was literally seeping from her head. Miraculously, she lived, but although the incident made it into the local papers, there was no mention of Judge Sebastian or his agreement to release the violent offender for several weeks. Several cops sent "anonymous" letters to the local newspapers advising them of his policy, but they were ignored.

It was Judge Sebastian who became the topic of conversation during the mental competency trial of Larry Evans. Most of law enforcement within the state of Ohio showed up to court to support the brutal murder of Mansfield police officer Brian Evans and were astonished when they learned that the prosecutors would not be arguing Larry Evans's "mental inability to stand fit for trial." This intelligent, sane, and cold blooded murderer was responsible for the murders of two people, the shootings of two others, and the attempted murders of nineteen police officers.

The case called for a three-judge panel that consisted of the county common pleas court judges to hear the testimony of various psychiatrists and determine whether or not Larry Evans was competent enough to stand trial. And it was Judge Sebastian who—halfway through the testimony, in front of a packed courtroom—fell asleep while seated at the bench. After all was said and done, the panel of judges ruled Larry Evans insane and ordered him to a mental institution until a doctor determined that he was fit to live among society. God help us all when that man gets out.

Judge Sebastian is just one example of a public official who abused his oath of office through the exercise of personal interest. In the case of another local judge (name withheld), religion carried more weight than anything else. This judge had battled the media and the ACLU for the right to display the Ten Commandments in his courtroom. He was extremely religious, and I had held him in high regard until a particular case of mine came before his court.

The state attorney general's office and state medical board had gotten hold of my agency in reference to a chiropractor who had been working without a license. In fact, this "pillar of the community" who had been operating as a chiropractor for over twenty years had nothing more than a massage therapy license. The state sent me in undercover with a camera in my purse to film the man performing chiropractic maneuvers on me. They had received a slew of complaints, including several stating that the man had caused them injuries resulting in a lifetime of complications.

The trial was pretty easy. After the jury saw my undercover video, and proof that the man had never attended chiropractic school, they found him guilty. It was only during his sentencing phase that I became concerned.

The man's attorney had clearly alerted him to the judge's religious beliefs. I had already known that the convicted man was rumored to be involved in a murder years earlier with a prominent physician and saw him for what he was—a piece of garbage. He stood before the judge, sobbing, insisting that his sole purpose in life was now "Jesus," second to taking care of his son. He told the judge that if he was a "God-fearing Christian man," he'd be lenient in his sentencing. The man further added, "Why should my thirteen-year-old son be punished for the sins of his father? Me!"

Incredibly, the judge relented (taken by the man's newfound friendship with Jesus, no doubt) and sentenced the man to probation. Apparently, the judge chose to forget about the numerous people who for years had suffered physically and financially at the hands of this man.

I realize it sounds as if I'm being completely negative toward the system, but truly I'm not. I just want everyone to know that in every village, town, or city in this country, injustice *does* occur—and we should all pay attention. I say this because it is the crime victims who are most important. Theirs are the voices that should be heard, that should dictate the course of justice. It's hard not to become arrogant in a position of power, but there comes a time when one needs to put aside pride and do what's right. Unfortunately, many officials would rather sacrifice someone else than do this.

The scariest part of this is that these instances of incompetence and lack of judgment are rarely exposed and dealt with. Anyone can file a complaint with the state supreme court or the bar association, but the vast majority of such complaints get swept under a pile and forgotten. The only solution for us, as a society, is to start truly paying attention to what goes on in our local courts. Start following cases and examine the outcomes; read the law and see if the judge follows the sentencing guidelines. Come elections, most people find it easiest to vote for the name they're familiar with (generally because of media or PR saturation), but what do they truly know about the candidate(s)? I'm not saying a particular judge or prosecutor alone is responsible for the plight of society or the crime rate in a particular city, but as a taxpaying citizen, you have the right—the responsibility—to examine the facts carefully and then vote for the people you feel will best fulfill these positions.

Throughout my career, I was never a huge fan of the media. I saw them as hound dogs looking to bring cops down, to focus only on the negative. Then, when I left law enforcement and became part of the media, I realized that they offer one of the few reality checks on the criminal justice system. The media can also be law enforcement's best friends—helping to find a suspect, showcasing an officer who goes beyond the call of duty, or highlighting an agency that truly works for the good of the people. However, the media can report only on what they have knowledge of, and in certain cases, that is very little.

In the last three years of my career, I made numerous arrests (specifically misdemeanors) but received only one court subpoena. This tells me that the city prosecutors either offered a plea deal, the suspect pleaded guilty, or the system threw out the case.

In their defense, the caseload for misdemeanors is overwhelming. There simply aren't enough municipal court judges to handle the number of cases, so they encourage plea deals. This is half the problem with the court system: overloaded, few prosecutors, few judges, and a financial inability to try the cases. It seems that society as a whole is suffering the consequences.

Every day in our country, there are countless cases of criminals who get what they deserve, go to prison, and will never again be a threat to society. Unfortunately, it takes only one case—one judge or one prosecutor who fails to fulfill his or her responsibilities in ensuring the rights of the victims or the victim's families—to forever alter one's perception of the criminal justice system. Prosecutors and judges are endowed with a public trust to further justice. For those who suffer at the hands of the few elected officials who betray this trust, I say:

Diligence is a necessity.

PART IV

Breaking Out

CHAPTER 14

Death Is Just Around the Corner

L IKE A LOT of other Catholics, I've had my share of uncertainties with the Catholic Church. Not enough to walk away and become a Scientologist, but enough to worry on occasion about suffering an undetected brain aneurysm or a heart attack. I hear that God is "kind and forgiving." Baptized and raised Catholic, I've formed the opposite opinion. And from a religious point of view, I feel as if I've been walking through life on pins and needles, waiting for the punishment I know is coming, and one that is probably deserved.

MY FATHER IS VERY devout. I could find more religious information from him than I could from any priest. Both my parents grew up in Catholic households and schools, but my mother's memories are less than pleasurable. For instance, one of them has to do with the time a nun joined her family for dinner and secretly peeked into her bedroom for the sole purpose of humiliating and degrading her in class the next day for what a slob she was.

My experiences and memories started early on, but the fear continues. Until recently, I had forgotten the "unbaptized babies go straight to purgatory" dictum. My youngest daughter, Jordyn, was almost five when I remembered it. Flying into a panic, I called the priest immediately to set up her baptism. Whew! Saved again.

As a cop, it's hard sometimes not to turn your back on God. There are days when I see young, senseless deaths, mourning parents, innocent children victimized, and I wonder, *Where is God now, huh?* I've grappled with this for years. My father, on the other hand, says God is what gets him through it all, and that's how he's survived forty years of policing. I can't say I've ever really turned my back on God, but I think I realize I need a little more insurance than just faith to survive.

I attended a somewhat modern Catholic church growing up. I say "modern" because I was an altar girl. Quite a feat, since it was the early 1980s, when most Catholic churches used only boys in that role. We attended our Catholicism classes on Wednesday nights, and there was one particular class that forever changed my outlook on religion.

We were being taught about Jesus dying for others to save them and how that's the way people are supposed to live: sacrifice. At the end of the class, we watched a movie that couldn't have lasted more than ten minutes. I remember it well. The movie began by showing a small home by a set of railroad tracks, and inside was a father and his beautiful blond-haired, blue-eyed, three-year-old little boy. They were playing and having a good time.

The phone rings. The father, a railroad worker, answers it and you can see his face go pale. The caller (his boss) tells him that one of the tracks has become dislodged and he'll have to manually pull a lever to even them out. He has to hurry because a passenger train carrying three hundred people is approaching. If the train hits the upended track, it will derail and plummet hundreds of feet over the bridge, killing everyone.

The father runs up to the tracks and grabs the lever just as the train is rounding the bend. Just then, the father hears his little boy calling, "Daddy! Daddy!"

His son, who unbeknownst to the father had been following close behind, is standing in the middle of the tracks. The father tries to call out to his son, but the sound of the approaching train is too loud.

For a few seconds, the camera closes in on the anguish in the father's face. Do I pull the lever and save the people? Or do I save my son? At the last second, he pulls the lever and his son is run over by the train, killed instantly. As the father holds the lever down, screaming, the camera pans to the inside of the train, where the passengers can be seen laughing and talking, unaware of the tragedy that has just occurred outside.

It was the most god-awful movie I had ever been forced to watch in my life, and I was only twelve. I don't think I slept right for weeks after. I understood the point of the movie, but showing it to kids?

Here's my point: Without a doubt, 100 percent, I would *never* have pulled the lever and let my child die. I'm sure there are plenty of churchgoing people who would be appalled by this, but I look at it differently. My opinion is that the track dislodged for a reason and those people's numbers were up; it was their time to go. God obviously made it that way, so who am I to interfere with it? And if that reason isn't good enough, then saving my own child's life is. The hell with everyone else. They may be Christians, but I'm sure most *parents* would agree with me. So am I wrong for not pulling the lever? Maybe, maybe not.

When you think about death, especially as a police officer, you realize that it can happen any minute, any second, of any day. Seeing a fellow officer killed or rolling up on a car crash and realizing the dead driver is a friend of yours is something that traumatizes you for life. It's amazing that someone can go from life to death in a split second; we just wink out. These are thoughts that began to keep me up at night. This was when I entered my "death mode" and started to take a good look at my career.

CHAPTER 15

Turning Point—Tactical Barbie Becomes Nancy Drew

I'M NOT SURE where in my career I hit a brick wall or began my "death mode," but it was somewhere around 2004. I still don't know why or how it happened, but it happened. It started out subtly and quickly grew into a monster.

One day in particular stands out. I was making a simple car stop, the guy took off, and a pursuit began. No big deal, I've been in plenty. But during this particular pursuit, something happened. As I was on the radio calling out my location, I noticed my heart rate was racing off the charts, I was on the verge of hyperventilating, and I had broken out into a sweat. This was not the typical surge of adrenaline we all get during intense calls—this was something else. In fact, when the other officers and I eventually got the car stopped, it was all I could do to maintain my balance when I got out of my car.

I immediately assumed I had gone into SVT—supraventricular tachycardia, a heart condition I have. For no reason in particular, my heart will fire another "electric" charge, causing it to pump at a horribly fast rate. It's not a terminal condition, just more of an annoyance. I take medication for it and see a cardiologist every two years.

After the pursuit, I immediately made an appointment with my cardiologist, assuming I needed a higher dose of the medication. When I spoke to the doctor, I explained what happened and said, "I can't have this happen when I'm working. It's too dangerous." Several tests later (which showed nothing wrong), the doctor prescribed the highest dose and basically said that it shouldn't happen again, but if it did, something else was going on. I later learned what an understatement that was.

Shortly after, I found myself reacting to calls differently. I started to get overly paranoid. Some say that's called being safe, but that's not what this was. I handled the calls as I always did, tactically and making safety my first priority, but it was my thought process that changed. Instead of thinking proactively, I was focused on a gazillion different scenarios of what "could" happen. I found that after I was finished with high-priority, dangerous calls, I was exhausted—physically and mentally. Was I actually getting scared? I didn't dare allow myself even to think it. The subject was taboo with officers. As long as I could put up a good front, everything would be fine.

Still, I knew I was feeling stressed and had to do something about it. Rich and I were in the process of building our new home, and since we had sold our other home much sooner than expected, we had to live in one of the extremely small rental properties we owned until school started in the fall. Then we'd have to find a house to rent in the district. Most of our belongings were in storage, and we were all tripping over one another. It was the summer of 2004, and that was the first time the notion of writing a book occurred to me.

In July, I received a very unusual call—an alert that had been sent out. A man was allegedly holding his wife and infant son against their will, driving around in his car with a stockpile of weapons. We had the description of the vehicle (bearing West Virginia license plates) and patrolled various areas looking for it. I headed for the Little Kentucky area of town and found the man pumping gas at a nearby gas station. I promptly called it in, walked over to the man, and placed him under arrest. The wife and infant were fine and were not being held against their will. It was at the station, during the interview with the man and his wife, that the "unusual" circumstances began to surface.

The man claimed he had become involved with some unsavory characters in West Virginia and had been running methamphetamines for them back and forth to Ohio. He added that the unsavory characters consisted of a few West Virginia locals and a corrupt sheriff's department. He made shocking statements about missing women there, claiming they had been killed by members of the sheriff's department or the locals all involved in the drug ring and even proceeded to give me a few names. He said that the suspects ate—yes, ate—one of the women. He said the reason he was driving around armed, with his wife and child, was that they were threatening all of them—and he was scared.

Obviously, I thought his claims utterly ridiculous, that he was just another scumbag criminal weaving a colorful story in an attempt to get himself out of being arrested. To prove him wrong, I excused myself and went into another room to do an Internet search of the West Virginia county and the names of the missing women. Sure enough, up pops a dozen or so articles about missing women in that area and claims of a large drug ring. An anonymous "witness" told the newspaper that she was present during one of the murders. They had actually put the woman through a wood chipper, mixed the remains, and eaten them. She said they called them "bitch burgers"— cooked them on the grill and all.

My stomach convulsed.

Now, I could have easily assumed the man had obtained his information from the news articles, but the problem was that some of the names he gave were not included there. However, I verified these names as being public officials in that area. And this area was extremely backwoods. Most of the people lived in the hills, in trailers, and were very poor and uneducated. It was an area known for high crime—those that were even reported—an area known as "Murder Mountain."

Deciding it would be best not to write off the man's claims as ridiculous (meaning I needed to cover my ass), I called a contact of mine in the FBI and told him the entire story. He had known several agents who had worked in West Virginia, and what he told me sent chills up my spine.

"I can't say that would be out of the ordinary down there, Stacy. Some of the law enforcement are just as criminal as the criminals themselves. Obviously, not all, just in the really rural areas. They get paid five bucks an hour and use their own cars to patrol; it's just a different world there."

We released the man on a misdemeanor charge, and I basically forgot about the whole thing—until September 2007, when the story of twenty-year-old Megan Williams hit the news. Megan was a young black girl who had been kidnapped by six white people. For over a week, they held her in their mountainside trailer. She was raped repeatedly, stabbed, fed rats, dog, and human feces, and tortured. It was one of the most horrific cases I had ever read about—and she survived. Just three days earlier, I had read an article about two young women kidnapped in Columbus, Ohio. Their perpetrators said they were taking them to West Virginia to be prostitutes.

At this point, there wasn't a doubt in my mind that the man's claims about Murder Mountain were true.

I used to drive through West Virginia on average of twice a year and truly appreciated the beauty of its mountains and landscapes. Unfortunately, I look at them now and think, *There are a lot of horrible secrets among these mountains...if people only knew....*

That day in July 2004, I went home after my shift with my head spinning, thinking about the man's claims. The next day was my day off, and Rich and I found ourselves in the rare position of having a babysitter. We decided to drive out to our construction site, build a bonfire in the front yard, and have a couple of beers. Our schedules at the time were pretty hectic, so we welcomed any time we had to spend alone.

It was the first chance I'd had to tell Rich about the events of the previous day. I gave him a play-by-play of the entire case and ended my story with, "I don't know if the guy is telling the truth or not, but this is one of those stories that would make a hell of a book!"

"You should write it," he said matter-of-factly.

I laughed at his joke. "Yeah, okay, I'll get right on it."

"No, seriously, you could write that. There isn't a doubt in my mind you could do it."

At the time, I thought he was nuts. What the hell did I know about writing a book? I was a cop, not J. K. Rowling. So I wrote good police reports, did exceptionally well in English while in college, had a vivid imagination, could tell awesome stories, and began reading when I was three years old. Did that qualify me to be a "writer"? Absolutely not!

I blew off the idea at the time, but I won't lie—the notion rattled around in my head for the next six months.

In mid-January 2005, we had just moved into our completed home and were recovering from a major ice storm that left us without electricity for two weeks. Not a winter person, I was walking around one day feeling as if I were going to jump out of my skin. Mentally cheering myself into it, I went to my computer, turned it on, and wrote the first five pages of my novel: Ace detective CeeCee Gallagher was born.

It took me a while to get the hang of it. I realized after sitting at a desktop computer for hours on end that a laptop would sure come in handy. After I bought one, I wrote with a fury. I was catapulted to West Virginia while CeeCee and her cohorts fought the bad guys. I began to realize what a stress reliever writing was for me. And at the time, I had never even given a thought to actually having the book published—I was just having fun writing the damn thing.

It was amazing, really. I could make these characters do whatever I wanted, say what I wanted, and dictate where they were going. As for CeeCee Gallagher, I made her into the cop I wished I could be. That was when I realized just how jealous I was of Rich professionally. Up until that point, I had never come out and said it, nor had I acknowledged it mentally, but it was true. I mean, seriously, he's my husband, so why in the world would I be jealous and not just proud? Good question. I was, am, and will always be proud of Rich. He's one of the best police officers I've ever known. But it was difficult sometimes.

I'd come home after a long day, spouting off about a particular case I had handled, and wonder why the outcome wasn't what I expected. He'd always listen, never interrupt or look bored, but hang on to every word. Regardless, every so often he would say calmly, "Why didn't you simply do..." and offer his opinion. I would stop talking, look at him, and think, *Why in the hell didn't I think of that? It's an obvious solution!* Then, of course, I would feel completely stupid (that was never his intention) and grab a bottle of wine. We would watch movies and I would try to get one up on him by predicting the outcome based on my "law enforcement experience." Here's an example:

"Oh, this is so predictable." I roll my eyes. "The guy is going to escape through the woods...."

"Of course he's not," says Rich.

"Of course he *is*!"

"Nah, the woods will be full of SWAT members...."

And what do you think the outcome of the movie was? You guessed it: The guy ran into the woods smack into SWAT members and was promptly arrested.

This is merely an example of what happens weekly when we watch movies or talk about current events. It's frustrating to me. There are only a handful of occasions where I've actually been right about something. It makes me wonder if our conversations and debates didn't somehow have an effect on me while on duty, undermine my self-confidence. I told this to Rich once, and he said I was being ridiculous, that I was a damn good officer. Still, where CeeCee Gallagher was concerned, she was always right, and that felt good.

People always ask me, "CeeCee is really you, right?" Wrong! When I created her, I was just beginning to suffer my mental paralysis on duty. I wanted a character who was stronger than me. Granted, CeeCee had a complex personal life, but her fearlessness, smarts, and confidence as an officer were enviable qualities that I could only hope for at that point in my career—I had lost all of it and didn't know why.

I remember reading a story by Stephen King where the main character was an author. The author dreamed of becoming the character in his books—a 1920s private investigator. Well, the author woke up in his character one morning.

I used to think that I'd give anything to wake up as CeeCee Gallagher (minus the marital and personal problems). It took me several years, five books, and retiring to put that wish into perspective.

Halfway through the first CeeCee Gallagher book, I thought, *This isn't too horrible; maybe I should consider getting it published.* From my long-ago days of modeling, I knew I had to get an agent first, and I knew the chances of getting published were slim. What never occurred to me at the time was that my "stress reliever"—writing books—was actually going to triple my stress levels. Why? Because I began to see writing as a way out; if I could get published, I would make millions, quit my job, have no stress, and live a great life. My naïveté of the process is laughable now.

I signed with my first agent in December 2005, after at least fifty rejections. The six months that followed put me in the best mental and physical shape I had been in for years. Call it inner peace or whatever, but I had found it. I quickly wrote the second book in the Gallagher series, lost thirty pounds, and did my job as a police officer in the best way I knew how. By the winter of 2006, I decided to switch agents and had received several rejections by publishers. I was becoming frustrated, and things began to go downhill.

The main problems started in my back and neck. I had never gone to a chiropractor in my life and found myself facedown on a chiropractic table twice a week. It got so bad that I was sometimes incapacitated for days.

After my second agent dumped me, I went into full-blown

overload. I was back to square one. The last two years of waiting and hoping for the chance to be able to work at home, spending time with my children—wasted. I would now continue to miss soccer games, school plays, trick-or-treat, and Christmas mornings. My oldest daughter was almost seven years old the first time I was ever able to take her to see fireworks on the 4th of July. Holidays like New Years Eve? I can't remember the last one where I wasn't sitting inside a police cruiser, ringing in the New Year with a bad cup of coffee and wishing I was out dancing the night away with my husband.

Looking back on the latter part of 2007, I realize I was nothing but a ghost. Not only were my back problems worsening, but I started to get horrible ulcers on the inside of my mouth and blisters on the palms of my hand, and at one point I began to find large clumps of my hair on the shower floor. Of course, I then convinced myself I was dying.

My chiropractor told me that I needed to do something about my stress before I wound up in the hospital. I blew him off and headed for my doctor, convinced something else was going on. A few ultrasounds and blood tests later, he informed me, "You're fine, you're entirely too stressed."

I blew him off, too, and headed for the cardiologist for another round of tests. "Your heart is as healthy as a horse," the cardiologist said.

Sometime around the period that Britney Spears shaved her head in front of the world, I found myself in a hospital emergency room. I had gotten off work and was getting undressed when I spotted a mole on my back, the same one I'd had since birth. Only now I thought it looked funny and I freaked, assuming it was cancerous and that was why my back hurt (I know, it's ridiculous). Imagine how I felt when the ER doctor came into my room and sat down. I remember what he said word for word.

"Never in my nineteen years as an emergency room physician have I had someone come in here for me to look at a mole at two a.m. You are a healthy thirty-four-year-old woman, and you are a basket case. In fact, you shouldn't even be working right now. You really, really need to make some changes in your life."

Easy for him to say. I had to work, and being a cop was all I knew how to do.

He wrote a prescription for Valium, which I promptly tossed aside for fear of winding up like Anna Nicole Smith or Elvis. I had a glass of wine instead.

Rich, who had been my rock through this whole nightmare—and had stood by silently—finally spoke up. Yes, he loved me with everything he had, but I had to make some changes, mainly for the sake of my kids. And he was right.

At the time, I refused to acknowledge that the root of the problem was my job. I told myself it was the dashed hopes of being published and the pipe dream that I would be able to stay home with the kids. Acknowledging that the problem was my job made me extremely weak, in my opinion. I had been working in law enforcement for fifteen years—my father was still going strong after forty years on the job, so why couldn't I handle it? I had to realize that I was not my father, I was not Rich, I was not the other officers I worked with, I was simply me.

And growing up looking at pictures of homicide scenes at

seven years old, reading about homicides, and spending my teenage weekends in a patrol car, followed by my own experiences as a police officer, had simply been too much. I was burned out, and that didn't make me weak. At that point, I did my best to get my shit together, and I prayed.

By October 2007, things started to turn around as far as my writing went. I got another agent, Claire Gerus, who put things into perspective for me and got me feeling positive about my future in writing. On the flip side, my job as a cop seemed gloomier with each passing day. I was constantly tired. I would work the two to ten p.m. shift, go home (passing Rich on his way to work the night shift), drive my babysitter home, put the kids to bed, and start writing. Most nights I stayed up until four or five a.m. writing my books. Fortunately, Rich got the girls off to school when he got home in the mornings, but living constantly on four or sometimes even three hours of sleep took its toll. Most of the guys I worked with knew I was writing. My circle of friends on my shift supported me, but there were others who simply rolled their eyes and laughed behind my back.

Mostly the problem was the internal bullshit that seemed to blanket every police department across the country. Politics, the blame game, and favoritism compromised the potential for advancement among the rank and file. After what I perceived to be a "block" by several union members to keep me from becoming a detective, I knew there was no hope. I could take the sergeant's exam, but then I would be stuck on the afternoon shift for more years than I was looking at already. I felt defeated, betrayed, and angry.

December 13, 2007, began like any other day. I went to work and found a little down time, so I decided to go to the jail and have my cruiser washed by the inmates. I was standing inside the garage talking to a few corrections officers when my cell phone rang. It was Claire.

We had just gotten an offer for a two-book publishing deal.

I started screaming so loudly inside the garage that I think I scared a few of the inmates back into their cells. It had finally happened, something I had worked so hard for.

I asked my supervisor for the rest of the day off and headed home to share the news with Rich. We used to spend hours fantasizing about what it would be like should this day come. We said we would celebrate with an elaborate dinner and an expensive bottle of champagne. When I got home that day, I told him I'd left work early because I wasn't feeling well. I gave it a few minutes (I was bursting inside) and then handed him a note. It read, "Well, I think it's time to buy that bottle of champagne now...." His reaction was funny. He kept looking at me and back at the note in disbelief. Eventually it sank in and he yelled as loudly as I had. The bottle of champagne we drank that night sits on my desk to this day, a reminder of hard work paying off.

As for the people who laughed and rolled their eyes? They didn't have much to say.

The advance on the books was pretty small, but I didn't care. I certainly couldn't quit my job, but things started exploding from that point on.

It was just a matter of time.

CHAPTER 16

Mommy's Home to Stay

WORD SPREAD PRETTY quickly about my publishing deal. I remember calling my father and hearing silence on the other end of the line. I wasn't sure if he'd heard me or not, but then I realized something else. My father had supported me 100 percent in my writing ambitions, but he'd known the chances were minimal that I would ever make a go of it. To him, it was like chasing a pipe dream, so now he was in shock. I couldn't help but laugh.

"You really did think I would actually be able to do this, did you?" I taunted.

"Of course I did, baby! It's just that the chances were so slim—but I knew if anyone could do it, you could!"

My mother cried, and my friends screamed. Shortly after the deal came through, I was offered another opportunity: A new crime blog called Women in Crime Ink wanted me be one of their regular contributors. Comprising top true crime and mystery writers, network journalists, and published attorneys, it was an amazing site and I was honored to be invited to join them.

I was still working at the sheriff's department at this point; I wasn't about to quit my job, because the advance on the book deal couldn't support us and I wouldn't see any royalties for at least a year after the first book's release. But then, as so often happens, things at work began to change—subtly at first, then more forcefully.

Colleagues and co-workers seemed to be treating me some-what differently—not everyone, just a handful, and certainly not on a wolf pack scale. Every once in a while, I'd be met with a dismissive or condescending attitude from a few people who used to be my good friends. At the time, I assumed they were having a bad day.

Then Nancy Grace called.

Her producers had found me through the Women in Crime Ink Web site and wanted me to appear on the show as a com-mentator. I had to reread the e-mail three times before I realized what they were asking. I was going to be on national television, and the thought both excited and terrified me. After I confirmed with the producer that I would be honored to appear on the show, I walked into the bathroom and looked at myself in the mirror.

It was not a pretty sight.

The past several years had definitely taken a toll on me. I had put on weight, I had stains on my teeth from drinking wine as a sleeping aid, my hair was two-toned from the awful amount of grown-out black roots, and my complexion looked like hell.

Realizing it takes only one opportunity to jump-start a life, I reached for the phone book and scheduled a series of "self-improvement" appointments: teeth bleaching—*check*! hair coloring—*check*! facial—*check*! There wasn't much I could do about the weight issue in two days other than order a pair of full-bodied Spanx through express mail.

The day of the show, I was a nervous wreck. I had scheduled an appointment to have my hair done and walked out of the salon looking as though I were going to a prom. I was starting to regret telling everyone I knew that I was going to be on the show. My local newspaper even did a small article about it, and I was getting flooded with e-mails that read, "We're having a Nancy Grace party with about twenty people tonight just to watch you!"

An hour before the car was scheduled to pick me up, I began to panic. The producers had e-mailed me a stack of documents on the show's topics. We were going to be talking about Illinois police sergeant Drew Peterson, who allegedly had murdered two wives, and a meth-addicted mom who put drugs in her toddler's bottle. There were at least one hundred documents on the Peterson case alone, and I had no idea what questions Nancy was going to ask me. During the car ride, I thumbed frantically through the pages, trying to familiarize myself with the basics.

After arriving, and while getting my hair touched up and makeup done, I began to get a familiar feeling in the pit of my stomach. By the time I was seated in front of the camera, I was almost in the throes of a full-blown panic attack. Since I was appearing on the show via satellite from a studio from Cleveland, I couldn't see anyone—not Nancy or any of the other guests. I was in a room with only the camera lady and had to sit there and stare directly into the camera for the entire hour, since I never knew when Nancy would cut to me. As the music began to play in my ear microphone, signaling that the show was starting, my heart rate went up about ten notches. All I could think about was all those people sitting on their couches, eating popcorn, and waiting for me to appear. Five minutes into the show, I realized I absolutely couldn't do it. *What the hell is wrong with you?* my head screamed. I had done television interviews before for the sheriff's department and had never experienced anything like this, and I didn't understand why I was going through it now.

Then it dawned on me: I was completely out of my element sitting there in that television studio. My life had been spent wearing polyester uniforms and gun belts, so when I did interviews for the sheriff's department, I was in familiar territory— the *Nancy Grace* show was definitely not familiar territory.

Ten minutes into the show, I was shaking so badly and having such a hard time breathing that the camera lady started drawing signs and faces to help me calm down. It didn't work. All I kept thinking was that I needed to get up and walk away now or make a complete ass of myself in front of the entire nation.

"Out to Stacy Dittrich, former detective and author of *The Devil's Closet*....Stacy, weigh in!"

Nancy's southern voice entered my ear, and I knew it was too late. I was definitely going to make an ass of myself.

"Thank you, Nancy! I think that in the case of Drew Peterson..."

I completed my talking points, and before I knew it, it was over. I looked at the camera lady, and she was clapping silently and gave me a thumbs-up. I don't know how, but I had gotten through it.

The next segment that I spoke on was significantly easier, and before I knew it, the producer came over my microphone, thanking me and telling me I could leave—the show was over. As I got out of the chair, I felt as though I had just been through a wrestling match; a mental meltdown can be quite draining. The camera lady began to laugh.

"I gotta be honest with you," she said. "You had me pretty worried there for a while. But when it was your turn, you just snapped right to it! Good job!"

As I left the studio, adamant that I would never put myself through that again, my phone started blowing up with texts and e-mails: "Great job! You were awesome!"

I smiled and hoped they had enjoyed it because that would be the last time I would ever appear on television. Or so I thought at the time.

Rich and the girls were waiting at the door when I got home. The girls were jumping up and down, so excited to have seen their mommy on television. Rich thought I did great, but because he knows me so well, he could see I was nervous in the first segment.

"It doesn't matter, because I will absolutely never do that again," I responded.

He laughed. "Oh, okay, we'll see!"

I went back to work after that and began to see the not-so-subtle changes. I was told that a few people I thought were friends were having a bitch session about my books and television appearance. Apparently, they felt that I didn't know any more than most cops and wondered what made me so special.

"They're absolutely right," I responded. "I *don't* know any more than most cops. But tell them to bust *their* ass for three years writing books, working full-time, and taking care of kids and actually get published. Then tell them to let me know when Nancy Grace calls them....I'll be sure to watch."

Sure, the minor drama died down after a short time, but I was becoming increasingly uneasy with my job. Toward the end, I had a fairly close call and almost got my clock cleaned, and I was tired of it. I was missing more soccer games and school plays—and, frankly, my daughters' entire lives. My agent had gotten me another two-book deal for true crime, and I was starting to feel overwhelmed. By the end of April 2008, I decided to come to terms with what was most important to me: my children.

Rich and I had a long talk and agreed that with my new book advances, it was time for me to take a leave of absence from the sheriff's department. Three months was about all we could manage, but it felt as though a ten-ton truck had been lifted off my shoulders.

For those three months, I was actually a mom. I worked on my books, took the girls to the swimming pool, attended soccer games, and saw the absolute joy on their faces when we were together. I hadn't realized how hard my schedule had been on them, and as it came time for me to return to work, they started to get upset. They needed their mom, and I needed them. Money or no money, it was time to make a life-altering decision. If I took an early retirement, I could use my pension to get us by for the next several years. It was certainly risky; we didn't know if I would be able to maintain a steady income after the money ran out. However, it was a risk we decided to take, and it was the best decision of my life.

I have to be honest: After I wrote my resignation and called the pension board, the resignation letter sat on my desk for almost a week. I would look at it and feel sick to my stomach. *Who am I if I'm not a cop?* It was a terrifying thought. Good or bad, law enforcement was the only world I'd known for my entire life. There were times when I'd look at normal (non–law enforcement) people and wonder what it would be like to see the world through their eyes; some days I actually wished for it. Maybe this would be my chance to find out—a fresh start, a new chapter.

When I was finally able to turn in my resignation, the sheriff swore me in as a "special" deputy right in his office. That meant I was still a sworn deputy and could throw on a uniform anytime I wanted if the urge hit me (it never has to this day). Also, I was still able to run the voice stress analysis tests for the department. It was the best of both worlds: I still had ties to the department, I could carry a gun and badge, and I could stay home full-time with my kids.

When I left that day, driving home, I had mixed emotions—I was relieved, sad, hopeful, and terrified. I didn't know what lay ahead, but I knew I had made the right decision. People say that God works in mysterious ways. This hit home when the events of the following year showed me just how lucky I was.

In September 2008, the bottom pretty much dropped out of the economy. I had received my pension money just two weeks before that, so who knows how much of it I would have lost had it been later. In March 2009, owing to the escalating meltdown, the sheriff laid off almost half the deputies, and it doesn't look as though they'll be getting their jobs back anytime soon. Bottom line is, I would have lost my job, and my family would have been in serious financial trouble. At the time these guys were losing their jobs, I had nine books scheduled to come out over the next four years, and although I'm certainly not a millionaire, I'm able to make a living out of it. It all worked out just fine.

I appeared on *Nancy Grace* again just two months after my first appearance. Okay, so Rich was right. In fact, I've done the show several times, along with hundreds of radio shows and newspaper interviews. Then Geraldo Rivera called, and then Bill O'Reilly. I can't say I don't still get nervous, but I've finally found my "niche." I've gone from being a cop to my new official title as author and law enforcement media consultant—and it's a title I've become comfortable with.

In all honesty, although there a few moments here and

there, I can't say I miss putting on the uniform or investigating cases. Life is too short not to live it to the fullest, something that's hard to do when you're worried all the time about making it home alive or wondering if your children will grow up without their mother. I worked hard for my achievements, and although a certain amount of luck is always involved in life, the hard work was key—and definitely worth the result.

Things are more hectic now than ever, but they're hectic from home, and that's what's most important. We still dream of a beachfront home in North Carolina, a dream where Rich can retire early and we can spend lazy days sipping wine and playing in the sand. As I write this from the balcony of our rented condo and look out over the ocean, I try to pretend that it's not just a vacation, it's our home.

Although many of my dreams have come true, I keep on dreaming...If we don't have our dreams, we simply have nothing.

ACKNOWLEDGMENTS

FIRST AND FOREMOST, my husband and daughters: Rich, Brooke, and Jordyn. When Mommy was writing this book, you all helped me more than you will ever know. I love you more than anything in the world!

Robin Sax, Claire Gerus, and Susan Murphy-Milano: You had the privilege of listening to my screams, cries, and tears and kept on me with your "You can do this!" when I said I simply could not finish this book. I owe each of you many bottles of wine.

My brother, Joe: Those childhood memories will never be forgotten.

Last, to my parents, Joseph Wendling and Susan Staral. I know it was shaky through some of those years, and I didn't always appreciate your advice and parenting, but I do now and realize I couldn't have asked for two more special people to guide me through life. Thank you, and I love you!